# LET'S
# TALK ABOUT
# **SEX**

**GLEN FARELL**

Dedicated to
*Drew, Aubrey, David,* and *Jesse*

May God keep your attention,
and may you live in love.

# TABLE OF CONTENTS

*For a spirit of whoredom has led them astray, and they have left their God to play the whore. They sacrifice on the tops of the mountains and burn offerings on the hills…Therefore your daughters play the whore, and your brides commit adultery. I will not punish your daughters when they play the whore, nor your brides when they commit adultery; for the men themselves go aside with prostitutes and sacrifice with cult prostitutes, and a people without understanding shall come to ruin. (Hosea 4:12-14 ESV)*

When Martin Luther posted his Ninety-Five Theses, he wanted to start a discussion about a few beliefs held by the Catholic Church. Luther was a priest, and he was saying, "Here I am, one of your own, and I want to talk about a few things I believe we have wrong." What drove Luther to do this is the same thing that is driving me today. The evangelical church, specifically the Southern Baptist Church to which I belong, is wrong. Luther did not wish to leave the Catholic Church but to improve and correct it. That is my goal as well. Unfortunately, the Catholic Church ended up excommunicating Luther, so I'm hopeful for a different outcome. However, staying silent is not an option. Now, without further ado, I say to my Southern Baptist Church community:

Here I am, one of your own, and I want to talk about a few things I believe we have wrong.

Have you ever discovered that you were wrong about something? I am betting there was a mix of emotions that came along when you realized the truth. Not long ago, my family had a gloves-off argument in the car. My wife, myself, and three of our four kids were adamant about the final score to a Texas Rangers game that we had been to several months before. However, David, our ten-year-old boy, disagreed with us. We took turns poking fun at him, and I took it as a teaching moment. I explained the importance of not holding strong opinions unless you know you're right and the importance of not arguing about those opinions unless you can defend them. After a good 15-20 minutes of arguing, my eldest son Drew had an epiphany. "Um, we have phones. Why don't we just look it up?" That was a great idea! Now we could cement the learning lesson for David, and I could end the day with a parenting success. It was going to be a great day. So Drew looked up the Rangers' score for the game we attended, and... oops. David was right. We were all dumbfounded. The car got silent, and to David's credit, he took his victory like the man I envisioned when I was offering my stellar parenting advice just moments ago. He said something like this: "Dad, you shouldn't hold strong opinions unless you know you're right. And you shouldn't argue about them unless you can defend them." Touche. My great parenting day turned into a lesson in humility. For me. I didn't follow my own advice, and as a result, I taught David the right lesson by accidentally demonstrating how NOT to behave. Over the course of the next week, there were three other examples of the rest of the family doubting David, and then finding out that he was right. Each time, I "knew" I was right, and ended up being wrong. By the end of the week, I had learned how to properly respond to him. And now, when we have a disagreement, I simply say, "Well son, I don't know for sure. Let's find out."

Let me tell you a little about me. I was raised in a Southern Baptist Church, with deep roots on both sides of my family. My mother's parents were Southern Baptist missionaries, and when their missions were done, my grandfather pastored multiple Southern Baptist churches. My father's parents were lifelong members of a small Southern Baptist church in rural Texas. My parents met at church in Dallas, Texas, and I grew up in that church under the pastoral teaching of W.A. Criswell. I was a Bible drill champion, attended church three times per week, and was heavily involved in visitations (showing up at people's homes to witness to them with the purpose of "winning" them to Christ). I signed the True Love Waits commitment card, vowing to abstain from sexual activity before marriage. I became a staff member and taught lessons to the youth group regularly. I then went on to get my bachelor's degree in Biblical Studies from The Criswell College. Until recently, my father was even the chairman of the Board of Deacons at a large Southern Baptist megachurch. I was completely immersed in Southern Baptist teaching: No dancing, no drinking, no cussing, no sex. The Bible is inerrant, you must walk the aisle, ask Jesus to come into your heart, and be baptized. Homosexuality is a sin, and those who practice it must be delivered from their evil ways. Masturbation is a sin, and you must refrain (this was taught at the True Love Waits conference for our youth group). Marriage is a Biblical institution defined by God in Genesis. Women should not be in a position of authority in the church. And all the other rules that you typically associate with evangelical Christianity, and more specifically the Southern Baptist Church. I took all the things I was taught for granted, never feeling the need to doubt or question what I learned. I am still a member of a Southern Baptist church, and I am still a devout Christian. However, my eyes have been opened to the faults and traditions that dominate Southern Baptist doctrine and thinking. I don't have a PhD, like most Christian authors, but I do have a strong understanding of Biblical interpretation, and I can communicate in plain language that hopefully will be easy for most to understand. While researching for this book, I read many other authors who agree with elements of what you will see here. But more often than not, I found myself skipping through their books, bored with the long-winded way in which the information was presented. I find that clear and simple is usually the best way to communicate. This book is not for the theological scholar. It's for the normal, church-going Christian who finds themselves immersed in a culture of tradition, trying to make sense of what the church claims is true knowledge.

The purpose of this book is not to condemn the Southern Baptist Church, or more broadly the evangelical church. Both are filled with loving individuals who are intent on doing the right thing. However, I do believe that the Church has been approaching the Bible and Christianity the wrong way. Long-held traditions are taking precedence over the teachings of Christ. Biblical interpretations are lazy and lack consideration for both ancient and current context and culture. The real purpose of this book is to encourage the Southern Baptist Church to lighten up on its condemnation of others and admit that it doesn't have all the answers. We need to have an open conversation about the current issues that divide the church, dive deep into scripture, and determine if it's time to change. The current state of the church is akin to the attitude I had in the car with David. I was adamant I was right until I was proven wrong. If I was honest with myself from the start, I would have admitted that I didn't know for sure, which would have led to less embarrassment for me and no need for correction from a 10-year-old. The Southern Baptist Church got its start in 1845 by believing that slavery was Biblical. That eventually led to the admission in 1995 that they had been wrong. What the church needs today is a 10-year-old to open their eyes. A plain-speaking, non-PhD, voice of reason.

I have decided to format this book in a way that logically and clearly addresses the main controversial topics that the Southern Baptist Church takes a firm stand on: sexual immorality, homosexuality, and marriage. How do we know that we are right? How do we know the knowledge we are claiming is, in *fact*, the truth, and why do we find it so important to be in possession of that knowledge? Does it bring us closer to God? Does it make us more righteous? Does God favor us because our beliefs are closer to the truth than others? And most important of all: ***What do we do if we find out we are wrong?*** I know you're eager to get to the part about sex, but we have some housekeeping to take care of first. We're going to start by exploring the Church.

CHAPTER 1:

# The Church

What is the church? Is it a building or a group of people? The short answer is yes, it is both, but it wasn't always that way. In Old Testament times, and well into the time of Jesus, the Jewish people used Synagogues. The Greek and Hebrew words for this mean "assembly" or "congregation." They could be tents or more permanent structures and were used for people to gather for communal prayer and to listen to readings from the scrolls. They were often used as the center for social life as well, where they would have school, hold court, or house travelers. They were not considered a place where God dwelled, as that was in the Temple, which could only be entered by a select group (Levites and priests). Jesus regularly taught in synagogues during his ministry. Fast forward to after the time of Jesus, and early Christians gathered mainly in homes. When Paul wrote his letters to the various churches (Corinthians, for example), he was writing to a community of believers in Christ from that region. Buildings built purposely for these groups to meet didn't come around until the late 300s when Christianity was legalized. When these groups would gather, they would partake of the Lord's Supper and collectively worship God through teachings, which were led by elders appointed by the apostles and their helpers (Acts 14:23, Titus 1:5). They took their instruction from the Old Testament scriptures as well as the letters and in-person instruction from Paul and the other apostles. While these early Christian communities (churches) did have elders, they did not have a pastor/lay people relationship. All men in the community were allowed to teach and prophesy in the church (I say men because the role of women was still very much restrained). The church communities took care of one another's needs, considering their belongings to not be their own. The needs of everyone were met by the community as a whole (Acts 4:32-35).

While a few church buildings were known to have been built in the late 200s, they were destroyed during the persecution of Christians. When Christianity was legalized and the Catholic Church established in the late 300s, large, elaborate churches began to be constructed. For over a thousand years, these churches were built by the Catholic Church using money it collected from tithes, tolls, marriages, and even selling the forgiveness of sins. People could pay to get a loved one out of purgatory, and could even put money into a savings account (called indulgences) which could take care of their past or future sins. The Catholic Church became very wealthy and powerful, involving itself in politics. The pope, in many circumstances, was more powerful than a king. People depended on the church for shelter, food, and protection, and the Catholic Church took advantage of that power. The size, wealth, and power of the Catholic Church became so large that some individuals began to speak up. Martin Luther spearheaded the Reformation in the 1500s, which resulted in the formation of Protestant denominations. While most Protestant denominations find agreement on the issue of salvation, they differ in many other areas.

The Baptist denomination maintained the belief in full immersion baptism (and a few other areas of disagreement with other denominations). The earliest Baptist church can be traced to the early 1600s in Holland, with John Smyth as its pastor. In the mid-1600s, the first Baptist churches were established in North America, in Rhode Island. Fast forward to 1845, when the Baptist churches in America split. The split began when the Home Mission Society (whose mission was to send missionaries to preach the gospel to the American frontier) decided to ban slaveholders from serving as missionaries. The Baptist churches in the South took issue with this, and the Baptist churches in the North agreed with the ban. The southern churches believed black people originated from Noah's cursed son, Ham, and they were therefore subject to the white man's authority. The churches split, and the southern churches formed an alliance called the Southern Baptist Convention. It is now the largest Protestant denomination in the United States. It wasn't until 1995 that the denomination formally renounced and apologized for its history of racism, slavery, segregation, and white supremacy.

Southern Baptist churches, in lockstep with most religions and denominations today, use a central building as a meeting place for their congregations. These buildings are paid for mainly using the tithes and donations of the congregations. They can range in size from just a few members to many thousands. While they are technically considered independent churches, they are bound by many doctrinal rules and regulations held by the Southern Baptist Convention. Though each church is technically independent, if a member church strays from the doctrinal opinion of the convention, their membership is revoked. Lately, several Southern Baptist Churches have been kicked out of the convention due to their acceptance of women as pastoral leaders or their acceptance of homosexual marriage. The churches are each led by a pastor, and there is a hierarchy of staff, all accountable to the Lead Pastor. Most have a board of deacons (or elders), along with stringent rules regarding eligibility to be a deacon (i.e some churches require deacons to sign a pledge to abstain from alcohol completely). Having received a master's degree in business, the structure today reminds me of a well-run corporation. You have a CEO, a hierarchy of employees, and a board of directors. Except, instead of funds coming from the sale of goods and services, they come from tithes (which, as good Baptist pastors will remind you, is a Biblical command).

In most well-established Baptist churches, the pastor is a career minister, holding no other job other than pastor of the church. He receives a salary from the church, as do the other members of the church staff. Church has become less of a community effort and more of a business. Rather than looking out for each other and using personal resources to fulfill the needs of our communities, members of the church write a check or submit a credit card to and expect church staff to care for everyone. The problem with this is that 50-60% of the congregation's tithes are going toward compensating the church staff. Add an additional 25% or more for admin, building maintenance, insurance, etc., and you're left with less than 25% of the budget able to be used for missions and ministry-related activities. Christianity Today surveyed 1,605 churches in 2014. They found, on average, only 18% of the funds coming into churches were used on missions and ministry. CDF Capital, a company that specializes in helping churches manage their resources, suggests that 5-15% of the church's budget be allocated to ministry-related activities, and 5-10% be allocated to missions. That means as low as 10% of the church's funds could be going toward meeting the needs of the congregation. Lifeway Christian Resources (the publishing division of the Southern Baptist Convention) in partnership with Guidestone Financial Resources (of the Southern Baptist Convention) publishes a compensation study regularly. In the most recent study, in 2022, the average salary of a pastor of a Southern Baptist Church in Texas, averaging over 1,000 in attendance was $187,000. If you add in health insurance and other benefits, the amount grows to $225,000.

Another problem with the business structure we have today is that the burden of ministry is unfairly placed upon the shoulders of the pastor. What was originally a community of believers in Christ, who saw to each others' needs, has become a membership-based club that pools its money in order to build and maintain facilities, expecting the paid members of staff to do God's work with the funds received. I am not attempting to discount the good that some of these churches do. In fact, I am quite proud of my personal church for their recent drive to pay off the outstanding medical bills of the people of my city. Members of the church donated $180,000 to the cause, which eliminated $19 million in medical debt. The donations amounted to $7,000 less than the average salary of a pastor of a church of this size. Just imagine what the church (meaning the community of people, rather than the organization) could have done if they weren't spending 50-60% of the budget on staff compensation. The ministers of the gospel during and immediately following the time of Christ were fed and housed by members of the church communities. However, they also had other jobs. Paul, for example, was a tentmaker. That's right, the man responsible for writing half of the New Testament had a job. Everything he received was a gift from people of the church, and not an expected salary. Don't get me wrong, I am not saying all staff members should be removed. There is nothing wrong with supporting a pastor or minister financially, or in other ways. In fact, that is exactly what the church communities did for the apostles. However, we need to remember that the work of the church should be a group effort. Ministers should rely on God to provide for their ministry needs through the community. When ministers rely solely on a fixed income, their priorities become skewed. With regular wages come expectations, which in turn cause ministers to watch what they say and abide by doctrines set by the denomination rather than Christ. Ministers of the gospel should be beholden to nobody except God. And we, as a community, a true church, have a responsibility to shoulder our share of the burden. We need to volunteer our time in order to cut down on the number of salaried staff members needed. I am the first to admit I could do a better job of this myself. We must partner with our church leaders, and provide for the needs of all in our community, including our teachers and ministers.

CHAPTER 2:

# The Bible

The following is an excerpt from the beliefs section on the website of my church:

> *The sole basis of our belief is the Bible, composed of the sixty-six books of the Old and New Testament, the Holy Scripture. We believe Scripture in its entirety originated with God (2 Tim. 3:16) and that it was given through the instrumentality of chosen men. Scripture thus at one and the same time speaks with the authority of God and reflects the backgrounds, styles and vocabularies of the human authors. We hold that the Scriptures are infallible and inerrant in the original manuscripts. They are the unique, full and final authority on all matters of faith and practice, and there are no other writings similarly inspired by God (Rev. 22:18). (https://www.hbcwaco.org/)*

You will find similar wording in most SBC church doctrines. The Bible is the sole authority upon which all beliefs are founded.

Scripture is infallible and inerrant in the original manuscripts. But how did we arrive at these conclusions? How did the Bible come about, and how do we know it is without error?

## History of the Bible

This is certainly not an exhaustive history, so for the sake of your sanity, here is a brief history of how the Bible came to be. The Bible is not one single book that suddenly materialized. It is a collection of writings spanning thousands of years, written by many authors, mainly in Hebrew or Greek (with some Aramaic as well). The first book, Genesis, is believed to have been written around 1400 BC, but we really don't know for sure. This was approximately 2500 years after the time the Southern Baptist Church believes the earth was created. Most scholars believe Genesis was written by Moses, but again, we really don't know for sure. However, Jewish tradition attributes the writing of the first five books of the Bible to Moses, so we will assume this is likely. The book of Genesis describes the creation of the world. However, again, Moses was not around for the creation of the world, so how do we know if he was accurate? Moses would have had to rely heavily on oral tradition and genealogies when composing Genesis. It makes one wonder how accurate he could have possibly been when relying on over 2500 years' worth of oral tradition.

Fast-forward to the beginning of the common era around the time of Jesus, when many other books of the Bible had now been authored. The Bible that was mainly used around that time was the Septuagint, or the Greek translation of Hebrew texts. It was translated by 70 Jewish Scholars somewhere between the 3rd and 1st centuries BC. When Jesus and the New Testament authors quoted scripture, they were often quoting directly from the Septuagint. We can assume that the apostles relied heavily on the Septuagint, which was the translation written in their language of that time, Greek. The Septuagint included all of the Old Testament writings that are currently found in western Bibles today. However, it also contained many more writings which have since been removed. These writings are what we currently refer to as the Apocrypha, seven of which are included in modern Catholic Bibles. Scholars believe that upwards of 50% of the Old Testament quotes found in the New Testament come directly from the Septuagint. If that is true, then the apostles held the Septuagint in high regard. So that brings up the question, why then does our modern Old Testament remove so many of the books found in the Septuagint?

Fast-forward again to 313 AD. By this time, the New Testament writings had been authored (somewhere between 40-100 AD). The Roman emperor Constantine issued the Edict of Milan. Up until this time, Christians had been heavily persecuted and outlawed. Constantine decriminalized Christianity, which then paved the way for Emperor Theodosius to establish Christianity (the Catholic Church) as the state religion of the Roman Empire. This allowed the Church to begin placing sanctions on fellow Christians who held different beliefs than the state. This was a time heavily influenced by Stoicism and Neoplatonism, and this is where the focus on sexual morality began. Many influential scholars at that time believed that sex was merely for procreation, and at its core was an evil activity. Notable scholars at that time were Jerome, Ambrose, and Augustine. Augustine is considered, even today, to be one of the greatest theologians of all time.

However, he was influenced by the idea of abstinence and believed the original sin was sex. He believed that sin passed to all, biologically, through the act of sex, equating sexual desire with sin. He is quoted as saying, "I don't see what sort of help woman was created to provide man with if one excludes procreation. If a woman is not given to man for help in bearing children, for what help could she be?" Ambrose earned the title "Doctor of Virginity" based on several books he wrote. While not discouraging marriage outright, he did hold the view that it is more virtuous to remain unmarried and chaste. Jerome maintained a very negative view of women, going so far as to say "Woman is the root of all evil." He also stated, "Do you imagine that we approve of any sexual intercourse except for the procreation of children? He who is too ardent a lover of his own wife is an adulterer." He believed that all sex is impure, and abstinence is the highest mark of the Christian. It was with these biases that Jerome translated the Old and New Testament writings into the Latin Vulgate. The Latin Vulgate became the official Bible of the Roman Catholic Church.

Fast forward to the 1300s, and we have Catholic Priest John Wycliffe. He questioned many of the Catholic Church's teachings and advocated for the Bible to be available in the language of the common people. He considered priests to be morally unworthy. He was responsible for translating the Latin Vulgate into English, making the Bible available to commoners. While little is known about his views on women or sex, he was a close follower of Augustine and was familiar with the sex negativity of the early church fathers. He remained a stout critic of the Roman Catholic Church, and 30 years after his death was declared a heretic by the church during the Council of Constance (1414-1418).

The council stated that Wycliffe's works be burned and his body removed from the ground. Thirteen years later, Pope Martin V carried out these orders, dug up the bones of Wycliffe, burned them, and threw the ashes into a river.

Moving ahead to the 1500s, we have Martin Luther and William Tyndale. Luther translated the Bible into German, and Tyndale translated the Bible into English. Luther translated mainly from the Latin Vulgate but also used the Greek. Tyndale translated from the original languages of Hebrew and Greek. Luther included the apocryphal books in his version but moved them to the end of the Old Testament, stating they were not equal to the sacred scriptures. Tyndale separated them completely, stating the apocryphal books were "uninspired." Less than 100 years later, in 1611, King James commissioned 54 scholars to translate the Bible. Those scholars relied heavily on Tyndale's English translation, and after several revisions and 6 years, the King James Version was complete (while it contained the apocryphal books, they were in a separate section).

Since that time, the Bible has been translated into over 700 languages, more if you count simply the New Testament translations. So, how did we, as Southern Baptists, arrive at the current makeup of our Bible? With so many scriptural writings in existence, why are some included and some left out of the Bible we use today? By the time of Christ, most if not all of the Old Testament canon had been established by the Jewish people. As discussed earlier, the Bible most used at the time of Christ was the Septuagint, which included the Apocrypha. The early church adopted the different New Testament scriptural writings little by little over the course of a few hundred years, and by 397

AD at the Council of Carthage, the New Testament had been "established." The New Testament was later confirmed at the Council of Trent in 1545. It's interesting to note that the Council of Trent was formed to counter the Protestant Reformation that was going on at the time, and while they allowed Protestants to attend, they did not get a vote. In addition to confirming the canon of scripture (to include the Apocrypha), here are some of the other findings of the council:

- The Church (Catholic church) is the ultimate interpreter of scripture (not the individual)

- Salvation requires faith AND works. They denied Luther's doctrine of justification by faith alone

- The grace of God can be forfeited through mortal sin

- The preference for celibacy was confirmed. If you were to get married, it MUST be before a priest and two witnesses, and if there is a divorce, neither party was allowed to remarry, even in the case of adultery.

So, in a nutshell, the books of the Bible (specifically the New Testament) were decided by men who believed the individual has no right to interpret scripture, and that you must be good in order to keep your salvation. Bonus points if you remain unmarried and celibate. The Bible as we know it was not presented to us on a silver platter. God did not give us a collection of 66 books and say, "Here is the rulebook for Christian living." The composition of the Bible we currently use was determined over a long history of time and is still debated even today. The New Testament did not exist during the days of the original Christians. Jesus did not tell us what writings to include, nor did he state the importance of adding new scripture. Once the writings had been established by the Catholic Church, they were then translated by men with biases. The main influencers and translators promoted celibacy as a means of obtaining a higher level of spirituality instead of enjoyment of sex. They also promoted the degradation of women. They were undoubtedly influenced by their own culture and beliefs when translating and interpreting scripture. And that brings us to the subject of interpretation.

## Interpreting Scripture

Words are funny. They're necessary to communicate, but they are finicky little buggers. Case in point, the word "bugger" can have several meanings, depending on where and when you live. It can be an expression of surprise, it can mean a small animal, it can mean "to leave", and it can mean a sodomite (or someone who penetrates the anus of another person). Look up the history of the word; it's quite amusing. Without an explanation of the word "bugger", someone reading this book could have interpreted my statement about words in one of many ways. In the same way, let's consider the word "gay." When one sings the popular Christmas song "Deck the Halls," there is a line which reads "Don we now our gay apparel." Does that mean to ditch the red and green Christmas garb and throw on some rainbow colors? Or take Fredrick Nietzsche's book *The Gay Science*. Are we to assume that science is attracted to members of its own gender? It sounds silly, I know. Of course, those examples are using a previous definition of the word "gay", which is happy, festive, joyous, etc. But how do younger generations know that? It requires explanation. And this is a word that had a different meaning less than 100 years ago, in our own language nonetheless. In 1938, Cary Grant improvised a line in his movie *Bringing up Baby.* He loses his clothes and is forced to put on his co-star, Katherine Hepburn's robe. When someone asks him why he's wearing a woman's robe he responds, "Because I just went gay all of a sudden." Since the line was improvised, there is no explanation of what the line was supposed to mean. People still argue today about whether he meant he was simply doing something frivolous, or if it was the first use of the word "gay" in film to connote something sexual. Let that sink in for a minute. This was an American film, less than 100 years ago, using an English word that has meant "joyful" since the 12th century. Yet, we can't properly interpret what Mr. Grant meant when he improvised his line. He passed away in 1986, and there is no record of him explaining what he meant in the movie. How then, can we be so certain that we are interpreting the words of Paul correctly when we translate his Greek word "arsenokoites" into the English word "homosexual?" There is no record of the word *arsenokoites* prior to Paul's usage, and most scholars agree that he coined the term. However, in 1946, it started being translated in English Bibles as "homosexual", including in the English Standard Version (currently used by my church), as well as in the New American Standard Bible. Like Cary Grant, Paul never had the opportunity to explain to future generations exactly what he meant to avoid confusion. We don't know what Cary Grant meant 86 years ago when he used an English word, yet we are certain what Paul meant 2000 years ago when he used an unknown Greek word (more on this word later on). A few other examples of how some English words have changed over the years:

- Naughty: used to mean "nothing," then became "evil or immoral," now it means "badly behaved."
- Awful: used to mean "worthy of awe," now it means "very bad or unpleasant."
- Silly: used to mean "blessed with worthiness," now it means "absurd or foolish."

Try reading the King James Version of the Bible today. You speak English, and it is written in English. Yet, you will find it very difficult, if not impossible, to understand some of the things you read. It's like watching a play by Shakespeare. Without an explanation of what you're hearing, you'll find yourself as lost as a ball in high weeds. Does your brain hurt yet?

You are no stranger to interpretation. Like it or not, you do it every day, in every conversation you have. Some things make it easy to interpret, such as your familiarity with the person you are communicating with, a shared vernacular, a similar upbringing or culture, body language, etc. However, at times, even with those you are closest with, misunderstandings happen. Those of you who are married know what I'm talking about, right? "Oh, when you said 'wash the dishes' you wanted me to dry and put them away too?" As difficult as modern marital interpretation is, interpretation of ancient manuscripts is so much more complex. First, you must translate the words from the ancient language to a modern one. Ask any translator today, and they will tell you how difficult it is to translate a modern language into another modern language, as some words have no equivalent in other languages. Add the complexity of an ancient language, and it becomes even more difficult. Once the words have been translated, you need to figure out what the author intended to say. This includes knowing the context of the whole situation.

- Who is the author, and what was their intention?

- Who is the audience?

- What was the culture like at the time of the writing?

- What were the current events, struggles, and general atmosphere at that time?

- When the audience heard or read the words of the author, what was their takeaway?

- Were the words meant only for the specific audience, or can they be applied to me today?

- Do the writings contain promises that I can claim as my own?

True understanding of a scriptural passage cannot be obtained by simply reading an English translation. This is the mistake made by so many pastors, authors, and church leaders. It's also the mistake made by parents at home when leading family devotions. Take my example of washing the dishes, for instance. If I had taken the time to ask my wife what she meant by "wash the dishes," I would have learned exactly what she had in mind when she asked me to do it. Just a little bit of research would have led me to a better understanding of what was expected of me. Interpreting scripture, of course, involves more time and effort on our part than simply asking the source, but it is nevertheless a necessity if we are to truly understand what is expected of us. And, as is the case with much of scripture, sometimes we simply need to admit that there is no way to know for sure how a passage relates to us today, in a different culture, at a different time.

Throughout this book, we will do some word studies using the guidelines listed above. As an example, we will now look at the word "adultery." The command to not commit adultery was given in Exodus 20:14 with the 10 commandments. There are two main words in Hebrew and Greek that translate into the English word "adultery." They are *Na'aph* (Hebrew) and *Moichos* (Greek). Modern English defines adultery as "sexual activity between a married person and someone other than that person's spouse." To find out what was meant by adultery in biblical times, we need to dive a little further. Vine's Expository Dictionary (a dictionary of New Testament words, i.e., Moichos) defines adultery as "unlawful intercourse with the spouse of another." So, what constituted "unlawful" intercourse? Let's look at the law they had at the time, from the Old Testament. Smith's Bible Dictionary says, "The parties to this crime, according to Jewish law, were a married woman and a man who was not her husband." Easton's Bible Dictionary states, "An adulterer was a man who had illicit (unlawful) intercourse with a married or a betrothed woman, and such a woman was an adulteress." Easton goes on to clarify that if the woman was not married, it was not considered adultery. The International Standard Bible Encyclopedia states, "In scripture, adultery designates sexual intercourse of a man, whether married or unmarried, with a married woman." It's interesting how with just a small bit of research, we already see a discrepancy between the modern view of adultery and the biblical view of adultery. It appears as though in Jewish law, it was only considered adultery if a married or betrothed woman was involved. This seems to be confirmed in some other scriptures on the subject.

- Leviticus 20:10 states, "If a man commits adultery with the wife of his neighbor…"

- Deuteronomy 22:22 states, "If a man is found lying with the wife of another man…"

To further understand this, we need to look at the culture of the time. In Old Testament times, the woman was considered the property of a man, whether that was her husband or her father. This continued well into and beyond the time of Christ (although Jesus did pave the way for equality of the sexes). For example, even in Jesus's time, only a man could divorce a woman, and not the other way around. They were still very much under Old Testament rule. Remember, the New Testament had not yet been written. For the Old Testament man, it was not considered adultery for him to have sex with a woman who was not his wife, provided she was not the wife of another man. In the case the woman is unmarried, yet still living at home, the man was simply required to pay the 'bride-price" and she would become his wife. If, however, the father of the woman refuses to give her as a wife, the man who slept with her still had to pay the "bride-price" and she remained the property of the father (Exodus 22:16). It is interesting to note that verse 16 is just one verse in a chapter full of laws regarding property rights. This follows the line of thinking of the commandment about coveting (Exodus 20:17), which lumps wives into the same category as real estate, livestock, servants, and "anything else that belongs to your neighbor." Adultery was considered the taking of another man's property without consent, something that belonged to someone else.

In addition to the culture of women as property, we must consider the issue of bloodlines. By having sex with a married woman, a man was in danger of impregnating her, which would pollute her husband's lineage. Lineage was of huge concern at that time because God had promised Abraham that the savior of the world would come through him (Genesis 12, Galatians 3). For that reason, the purity of the 12 tribes was extremely important. They believed that a bloodline passed through the father. Therefore, if a wife were to get pregnant by someone other than her husband, then the line would be polluted. In the same way, if a man failed to have a son during his life, then his bloodline would end. This is why another law (Levirate Marriage) mandated that if a man died without an heir (male offspring), then his brother must take the widow as his wife and have sex with her until she bears a son. That son will be considered the offspring of the dead brother, and not of the actual biological father (Deuteronomy 25:5-10). Lineage was to be protected at all costs.

So we see now that adultery was less about sexual relations and more about property rights and pure bloodlines. To confirm this, we have many examples throughout scripture of sexual relations outside of marriage which were not considered adultery:

- Genesis 38 - Judah and Tamar, a lovely read

- Genesis 35:22 - Reuben had sex with his father's concubine

- 2 Samuel 12:8 - God gave David the wives of Saul

- Deuteronomy 20:14 (and 21:10-14 )- God gives the Israelites women as plunder of war

- Song of Solomon 2:3 - During their courtship, she performs (and rather enjoys) oral sex on Solomon.

- Multiple mentions of men having concubines. Some argue that a concubine is simply a secondary wife, but concubines were not allowed to marry, and were not considered full wives at the very least. It was also not considered adultery to have sex with a concubine. There are many mentions in the bible that differentiate between wives and concubines (2 Chronicles 11:21 for example):

*Rehoboam loved Maacah the daughter of Absalom above all his wives and concubines (he took eighteen wives and sixty concubines, and fathered twenty-eight sons and sixty daughters)* (2 Chronicles 11:21 ESV)

So, considering what we now know regarding "Adultery," let's see how the context helps us understand scripture a little better. The audience for the laws regarding adultery was the Jewish people. Their culture was one of preserving their lineage, which was passed on through the male. The laws concerning adultery were designed to prevent men from tainting the bloodlines of other men. It involved sex only in the sense that sex is the means to procreation. Taking another man's wife was considered theft of property and was outlawed as a result. How do we apply this knowledge to the situations we encounter in today's culture? That is where this gets confusing. Knowing the specifics of what was meant by "Thou shalt not commit adultery" does not excuse having sex with someone other than your spouse today. Yet, at the same time, we can't point to Exodus 20:14 as the reason why it is not okay. The goal here is to make you think. Why do we believe what we believe about Adultery? Why do we translate the Hebrew and Greek words to an English word that implies all sex outside of your own marriage is against God's law? Is it not misleading when someone reads or teaches from the English translations and applies it to our culture today? For example, if a married man today has sexual relations with an unmarried woman, is he in violation of the biblical command in Exodus? Or is he, instead, in violation of a much simpler command given later on by Jesus when He said to love others? Cheating behind your spouse's back is certainly not the loving thing to do. Perhaps we should be approaching what we define as adultery from another angle.

Scriptural interpretation, as you can see, is not a simple task. We must dive into the dirty details of culture, context, and word meanings (which change over time even within a culture). Is it possible we could get it wrong even after careful consideration of word meanings and context? Of course it is, especially after thousands of years have passed. Sometimes, the best course of action is to just admit that the truth of a matter is beyond our reach. Instead of hanging our hat on a specific interpretation and preaching it as fact, it may be best to throw our hands in the air and say, "We don't know." But I'm not done with the Bible just yet. Remember the belief statement I took directly from my church's website?

*The sole basis of our belief is the Bible, composed of the sixty-six books of the Old and New Testament, the Holy Scripture. We believe Scripture in its entirety originated with God (2 Tim. 3:16) and that it was given through the instrumentality of chosen men. Scripture thus at one and the same time speaks with the authority of God and reflects the backgrounds, styles and vocabularies of the human authors. We hold that the Scriptures are infallible and inerrant in the original manuscripts. They are the unique, full and final authority on all matters of faith and practice, and there are no other writings similarly inspired by God (Rev. 22:18).*

I want to talk about a little sentence in here: *We hold that the Scriptures are infallible and inerrant in the original manuscripts.*

## Biblical Inerrancy

Let's begin by defining a couple of words. "Infallible" means "incapable of making mistakes or being wrong," and "inerrant" means "free from error." Belief in biblical inerrancy means that you believe the Bible is incapable of being wrong. It is without error in all its teachings. The belief in biblical inerrancy was held by various church leaders, such as Augustine and Jerome. However, others weren't so clear on the matter. Martin Luther believed there were numerous errors in scripture, but none that touched at the heart of the gospel. The jury is out on whether or not John Calvin believed in inerrancy. Some church leaders, both past and present, believe in inerrancy but allow for inconsistencies, citing personality differences in the authors. There is no record of inerrancy becoming church doctrine until fairly recently, in the last couple of hundred years. It is a multifaceted, complex discussion that would take forever to hash out in complete detail.

So, why does inerrancy matter? Most people who hold to inerrancy state that if the Bible contained errors, then there would be no way for us to know the truth, and thus truth would be otherwise unreachable. I do agree that there is merit to that logic; however, I would pose the question: why do we need to know the truth? Belief in Jesus Christ as savior is an act of faith. Faith, in its essence, is the belief in something that can't be proven. Even the Bible itself, in Hebrews 11:1-3, explains:

*Faith is the assurance of things hoped for, the conviction of things not seen. For by it the people of old received their commendation. By faith we understand that the universe was created by the word of God, so that what is seen was not made out of things that are visible. (ESV)*

Consider also Romans 1:16-17:

*For I am not ashamed of the gospel, for it is the power of God for salvation to everyone who believes, to the Jew first and also to the Greek. For in it the righteousness of God is revealed from faith for faith. As it is written, "The righteous shall live by faith." (ESV)*

The "gospel," simply defined, is the good news of Jesus Christ and who he is. Another way to translate "from faith for faith" is "beginning and ending in faith." So we could reread this text as follows: "I am not ashamed of the good news of Jesus, for in that good news, the righteousness of God is revealed beginning and ending in faith.

Our determination as Southern Baptists (not exclusive to other Protestant denominations) to be right in every doctrine is the opposite of faith. If we claim the Bible is without error and absolutely true in everything it teaches, then that means we take it as fact. And facts can be proven. Belief in a fact is not faith. Our goal then becomes, as good Baptists, to convince others of this fact rather than to spread the good news of Christ and let others decide whether or not to believe.

Let's return to my church's statement of belief. The vast majority of Southern Baptist churches have a similar statement. The question I pose now is, "How do we know the Bible we have today is inerrant?" There are three elements of the statement of belief that give me concern. The first is the fact that the church uses scripture to prove scripture is inerrant. In other words, "It must be, because it says it is." The church uses 2 Timothy 3:16, from a letter the apostle Paul wrote to Timothy. We'll discuss the details of this verse in a minute, but for now, we will assume that the verse says all scripture is inerrant. Can we then say, "Well, Paul says the Bible is inerrant, so therefore it is?" If a politician gives a speech, then claims that everything they said was true, do we take them at their word? Does a judge believe a defendant is innocent simply because he claims to be? If so, then you should believe I am the fastest human being on earth, because I am. We can't simply use the Bible to prove the Bible. Proof requires external evidence.

The second issue I have with the statement of belief is the content and context of the verse itself. 2 Timothy 3:16-17 states:

> *All scripture is breathed out by God and profitable for teaching, for reproof, for correction, and for training in righteousness, that the man of God may be complete, equipped for every good work. (ESV)*

Remember our earlier discussion on interpretation? To understand this passage, we need to understand what the author intended when he originally wrote it. The Greek word translated in the English Standard Version (ESV) as "breathed out by God" is *theopneustos*. This word is widely believed to mean "inspired by God" or "God-breathed." It's more likely that this passage means that scriptures are inspired by God, rather than suggesting they are without error. Many translations use the word "inspired" in their renditions, such as the King James Version, the New American Standard, and the New Revised Standard. The Southern Baptist Church takes this a step further and asserts that God is without error; therefore, anything inspired by Him is also without error. Does that mean that scripture is inerrant?

The next aspect we need to consider in this passage is what Paul meant by "scripture." At the time Paul wrote this verse, the New Testament as we know it did not exist. The Bible Paul used was what we now refer to as the Old Testament. I have two points here. First, the Old Testament that Paul quoted from so often was the Septuagint, which contained the apocryphal books. If Paul was stating that all scripture was inerrant, then why did we remove some of the scripture that he was referring to? Second, one would assume that if Paul wanted to make it clear that the letter he was writing to Timothy was to be considered inerrant, then he would explicitly state so. However, a look at the verse immediately preceding this passage provides us with some insight into what "scripture" he was referring to. 2 Timothy 3:15 states:

> ...*from childhood you have been acquainted with the sacred (hieros) writings, which are able to make you wise for salvation through faith in Christ Jesus. (ESV)*

Paul's reference to the "sacred" (*hieros*) writing in 2 Timothy 3:15 denotes the Old Testament scriptures. The writings Paul was referring to were the Old Testament. Timothy would have been acquainted with the Tanakh (Hebrew Old Testament) and the Septuagint (the Greek translation of the Hebrew Old

Testament). If Paul meant to include anything else, one would think he would have been more clear. Opponents of this view point out that Paul had previously written to Timothy in his first letter and referred to the gospel of Luke as scripture. In addition, Peter referred to Paul's writings as scripture in 2 Peter 3:15-16. However, upon closer examination of the word we translate as "scripture," the Greek word *graphe,* we see that it simply means "a writing, a thing written." Regardless of where you stand on this 2 Timothy debate, you can find evidence to support both an Old Testament or New Testament-inclusive option. Sometimes, the best course of action is to admit that the truth of a matter is beyond our reach. Instead of hanging our hat on a specific interpretation and preaching it as fact, it may be best to throw our hands in the air and say, you guessed it, "We don't know."

The third concern I have about the statement of belief is with the four clarifying words "in the original manuscripts." In fairness to the church, this is not something they invented. In 1978, over 200 evangelical leaders met in Chicago to discuss and clarify their stance on Biblical inerrancy. Among the signers of this declaration was my own pastor, W.A. Criswell. He was the man who sat me down in his office after I "walked the aisle," and confirmed that I had indeed invited Jesus into my heart. He sealed the deal by presenting me with a signed copy of *The Criswell Study Bible* (which I still have on my bookshelf at home). In article X of the *Chicago Statement on Biblical Inerrancy,* the authors state:

> *We affirm that inspiration, strictly speaking, applies only*
> *to the autographic text of Scripture, which in the providence*
> *of God can be ascertained from available manuscripts with*

*great accuracy. We further affirm that copies and transla-
tions of Scripture are the Word of God to the extent that they
faithfully represent the original.*

*Autographic* means "written in the author's own handwrit-
ing." In short, the inspiration (and as a result, inerrancy) are only
found in the original texts. They believe the texts we have today
are pretty close, but we really don't know that for certain because
the original manuscripts do not exist. Let me emphasize that
once more to let it sink in: the original manuscripts DO NOT
EXIST. If God wanted us to have an error-free rulebook to live
by, wouldn't He have made sure they were available to us? There is
not one single original manuscript from any of the 66 books that
are currently in our Bible. On top of that, we wouldn't know it
even if we found one. So our claim as a Southern Baptist Church
that *We hold that the Scriptures are infallible and inerrant in the
original manuscripts* means what, exactly? It means that the Bible
you hold in your hand when you sit down at a Southern Baptist
Church is not inerrant. The English versions are not inerrant.
The various scrolls in Hebrew and Greek are not inerrant. Only
the originals, not in existence, are inerrant. At this point, every
other concern we have about inerrancy doesn't matter. Because if
you read the fine print, we don't (and never will) have access to
inerrant scripture anyway. But it's pretty close…

## Conclusions on the Bible

So what is the takeaway here? Are we to discount the Bible as
an outdated collection of ancient writings? I don't believe so, and
here is why. Books are useful. All books are useful. We can learn

from them, we can teach from them, and we can be corrected by them. Does that sound familiar?

*All scripture is inspired by God and beneficial for teaching, for rebuke, for correction, for training in righteousness.*
*2 Timothy 3:16 (NASB)*

We can also critique them, to determine what is good.

*Test everything; Hold fast what is good.* 1 *Thessalonians 5:21 (ESV)*

The scriptural writings in our Bible were written by people who walked with God, some of them quite literally. They knew Jesus Christ, and they wrote about what he said, who he was, and they witnessed it all firsthand. How amazing that we have access to their writings today. I do believe they were inspired by God, and their writings are useful. Whether or not the writings are inerrant, to me, does not change a thing. My faith is only enhanced, knowing that I am making a *choice* to believe, not that scripture is inerrant, but that Jesus was who he said he was, did what the witnesses said he did, and is now the source of my salvation. My faith comes from something I can't prove, not from something the Church has declared fact. The Hebrew and Greek words we will be translating and interpreting throughout the rest of this book are closer to the original manuscripts than the Bible you hold in your hand. Keep an open mind, and test what you read.

CHAPTER 3:

# Perspective

Douglas Adams, the author of *The Hitchhiker's Guide to the Galaxy*, tells a funny story about something he experienced while sitting at the Cambridge train station in the UK. He went to catch a train, but arrived at the station early. He grabbed a newspaper, some coffee, and some cookies, and went to sit down. He laid everything down on a table and got settled in. There was a man sitting across from him, and after a few minutes, that man reached over, grabbed Douglas's pack of cookies, opened them, and took one out. Douglas watched as the man ate his cookie. He couldn't believe what was happening. He decided to take one of his cookies and eat it too, hopefully making the other man realize his mistake. After eating his cookie, the other man reached over again and took another one. They started taking turns eating the cookies until the package was empty. The strange man looked at Douglas, Douglas returned the look, and the man walked away. A little while later, the train pulled up, and Douglas got up, grabbed his coffee, picked up his newspaper, and underneath saw an unopened package of cookies. He finishes his story amused by the fact that somewhere out there, someone has the exact same story as him; they're just missing the punch line.

This story perfectly illustrates the need to be careful about our assumptions. Before we declare that we are right about something, we need to check under our newspapers so we can view a situation from the correct perspective. If we don't, then we may misunderstand something important. To understand the next several chapters of this book, you will need to approach it from the correct perspective. The Southern Baptist Church, and many other denominations, make declarations about certain beliefs according to their understanding of sin. Their interpretations of certain passages are viewed through the lens of what they believe is sin. So, before we continue, let's answer this question: **What is sin?** If you ask the church I grew up in, or the one I attend now, they would say "disobedience toward God." However, they would then go on to make a list of everything that qualifies. The list would include such things as lying, murder, worry, sex before marriage, lust, homosexuality, and many others. However, defining sin is not as specific as some would lead you to believe. The Oxford dictionary defines sin as "An immoral act considered to be a transgression against divine law." You can find a similar definition among evangelical sources. Most sources I found agree that sin is a transgression against God's law. We really don't need to look further than scripture for that definition. 1 John 3:4 states "Sin is lawlessness." And we know based on the words of Jesus, that you can be guilty of this lawlessness by thought and words, not just action. Jesus makes this clear in Matthew 5:21-30 when giving his sermon on the mount. He explains that simply being angry with a brother, or insulting him makes you liable, and looking with the lustful intent to commit adultery makes you guilty. So, then our definition of sin becomes *any thought, action, or word that transgresses God's law*. In order to understand this more fully, we then ask, "what is God's law?"

The Sadducees and Pharisees were two different Jewish sects with disagreements about various issues. However, they were both threatened by the ministry of Jesus and were intent on catching him in a mistake. The apostle Matthew recounts a situation in which the Sadducees told Jesus a story about a man who had seven brothers. The man died, meaning his brothers had to marry his widow in order to provide an offspring. One by one, each brother married the widow, and died before offspring could be produced. The Sadducees asked Jesus, "In the resurrection, whose wife will she be? For they all had her." Jesus's answer turned the tables on them as he declared people won't be given in marriage after the resurrection because they will be like the angels in heaven. Once the Pharisees heard about this, they took it as an opportunity for them to attempt to trip up Jesus as well (Matthew 22). They gathered together, plotted, and got one of them, a lawyer nonetheless, to ask Jesus a question. He asked, "Teacher, which is the greatest commandment in the law?" Jesus answered, "You shall love the Lord your God with all your heart and with all your soul and with all your mind. This is the great and first commandment. And a second is like it: You shall love your neighbor as yourself. On these two commandments depend all the Law and the Prophets." The apostle Mark (Mark 12) recounts the same situation but details that this Pharisee was a scribe, a lawyer whose job was to copy the scriptures. Nobody knew the law better than the scribes. Mark details this scribe's answer to Jesus. He said, "You are right, Teacher…to love him with all the heart and with all the understanding and with all the strength, and to love one's neighbor as oneself, is much more than all whole burnt offerings and sacrifices." Jesus replied to him, "You are not far from the kingdom of God."

I consulted various Bible commentaries to get their take on this passage (Matthew 22:34-40). Bear with me, as some of them are lengthy, and dare I say, boring. But they are necessary to see that the Church's understanding of the law is in tune with where I am going here.

Smith's Bible Commentary states:

> *The law was set forth in negatives. Thou shalt have no other gods. Thou shalt not, thou shalt not.* **Jesus put it in a very positive way, just love God with all your heart, soul, mind, strength, love your neighbor as yourself. And this is the law.** *This is basically what the law is declaring, that we should have a loving relationship with God first; that is reflected in a loving relationship with fellow man. This is what the whole Old Testament was all about; the law and the prophets hang on these two.*

Matthew Henry's Commentary states:

> *Observe what the weight and greatness of these commandments is (v. 40); On these two commandments hang all the law and the prophets; that is,* **This is the sum and substance of all those precepts relating to practical religion**

*which were written in men's hearts by nature, revived by Moses, and backed and enforced by the preaching and writing of the prophets. All hang upon the law of love*; take away this, and all falls to the ground, and comes to nothing. *Rituals and ceremonials must give way to these, as must all spiritual gifts, for love is the more excellent way.* This is the spirit of the law, which animates it, the cement of the law, which joins it; it is the root and spring of all other duties, the compendium of the whole Bible, not only of the law and the prophets, but of the gospel too, only supposing this love to be the fruit of faith, and that we love God in Christ, and our neighbour for his sake. All hangs on these two commandments, as the effect doth both on its efficient and on its final cause; **for the fulfilling of the law is love (Rom. 13:10) and the end of the law is love, 1 Tim. 1:5**. The law of love is the nail, is the nail in the sure place, fastened by the masters of assemblies (Eccl. 12:11), on which is hung all the glory of the law and the prophets (Isa. 22:24), a nail that shall never be drawn; for on this nail all the glory of the new Jerusalem shall eternally hang. Love never faileth. **Into these two great commandments therefore let our hearts be delivered as into a mould; in the defence and evidence of these let us spend our zeal, and not in notions, names, and strifes of words, as if those were the mighty things on which the law and the prophets hung, and to them the love of God and our neighbour must be sacrificed; but to the commanding power of these let everything else be made to bow.**

David Guzik's Study Guide states:

> *God's moral expectation of man can be briefly and powerfully said in these two sentences.* **If the life of God is real in our life, it will show by the presence of this love for God and others.**

Barnes' Notes on the Bible states:

> *On these two commandments hang - That is, these comprehend the substance of what Moses in the law and what the prophets have spoken. What they have said has been to endeavor to win people to love God and to love each other.* **Love to God and man comprehends the whole of religion, and to produce this has been the design of Moses, the prophets, the Saviour, and the apostles.**

Pulpit Commentary states:

> *Hang all the Law and the prophets; i.e. all Scripture, which is comprised in these terms; in other words, all the revelations which God has made to man in every age. The clause is peculiar to St. Matthew.* **It signifies that on love of God and love of man depend all the moral and religious, ceremonial and judicial precepts contained in the Law, all the utterances of the prophets, all the voices of history.** *Scripture enunciates the duty to God and our neighbour, shows the right method of fulfilling it, warns against the breach of it, gives examples of punishment and reward consequent upon the way in which the obligation*

*has been treated. Thus the unity and integrity of revelation is demonstrated. Its Author is one; its design is uniform; it teaches one path, leading to one great end.*

Matthew Poole's Commentary states:

*On these two commandments hang all the law and the prophets:* **there is nothing commanded in all the Old Testament but may be reduced to these two heads***. This is the whole duty of man there commanded. The whole book of God is our rule, and we are obliged to every precept in it. Moses summed up all in the ten commandments, to which, truly interpreted, all the precepts of Scripture are reducible.* **Christ here brings the ten to two. The apostle (Paul in Romans 13) brings all to one, telling us love is the ful-filling of the law.** *There is nothing forbidden in Scripture but what offends the royal law of love, either to God or man; there is nothing commanded but what will fall under it.*

Wow! So, Jesus was saying that all of the law, everything in scripture, from Moses to the prophets, to Jesus Christ, to the apostles, all led to these two commands: to love God and to love others. Moses reduced the whole of scriptural law into ten commandments. Jesus reduced it to two. And the apostle Paul reduced it to one. Paul states, in Romans 13: 8-10:

*Owe no one anything, except to love each other, for the one who loves another has fulfilled the law. For the com-mandments, "You shall not commit adultery, You shall not murder, You shall not steal, You shall not covet," and any other commandment, are summed up in this word: "You shall love your neighbor as yourself." Love does no wrong to a neighbor; therefore love is the fulfilling of the law. (ESV)*

And again in Galatians 5:13-14:

*For you were called to freedom, brothers. Only do not use your freedom as an opportunity for the flesh, but through love serve one another. For the whole law is fulfilled in one word: "You shall love your neighbor as yourself." (ESV)*

Paul also states, in his letter to Timothy (1 Timothy 1:5-7):

*The aim of our charge is love that issues from a pure heart and a good conscience and a sincere faith. Certain persons, by swerving from these, have wandered away in vain discussion, desiring to be teachers of the law, without understanding either what they are saying or the things about which they make confident assertions. (ESV)*

The law, according to scripture, is to love God and love others. Plain and simple. When speaking to Timothy, Paul states that the law was meant for the lawless (1 Timothy 1:9). To paraphrase, then, the law, which tells us to love, was meant for the lawless, those who do not love. We, as the Southern Baptist Church, have "wandered away in vain discussion," wanting to define the law and condemn specific sins, but we don't understand what we are saying, about which we make "confident assertions." If sin is lawlessness, and lawlessness is being unloving, then sin must therefore be defined as *any thought, action, or word that is unloving toward God or others.* Is what you are doing unloving? If so, then it is sin. If you are not being unloving, therefore, you are not sinning. Some excerpts from 1 John 3-4:

> *For this is the message that you have heard from the beginning, that we should love one another.*
>
> *Whoever does not love abides in death.*
>
> *Let us not love in word or talk but in deed and in truth.*
>
> *And this is his commandment, that we believe in the name of his Son Jesus Christ and love one another, just as he has commanded us.*
>
> *Beloved, let us love one another, for love is of God, and whoever loves has been born of God and knows God. Anyone who does not love does not know God, because God is love.*
>
> *Beloved, if God so loved us, we also ought to love one another. No one has ever seen God; if we love one another, God abides in us and his love is perfected in us. (ESV)*

ALL of scripture hangs on the commands of Jesus Christ. So, when we interpret the scriptures to determine what they say and how they relate to our culture and our lives today, we MUST weigh our interpretations through the perspective of Jesus Christ. If Douglas Adams had weighed the stolen cookie situation against the knowledge that they weren't really his cookies, then his perspective of the situation would have been completely different. We must weigh our understanding of scripture against the knowledge that Jesus calls us to love God and others, and nothing else. If an act is loving, then it can't be a sin.

Let me give you a practical example. Most Christians today would state that lying is a sin. Proverbs 26:28 says, "A lying tongue hates its victims." If it hates its victims, then it is clearly unloving, and therefore a sin. However, what happens when my wife walks in with a new outfit and asks me how it looks? Do I tell the truth, that the dress makes her otherwise gorgeous hind end look a tad droopy? Or do I tell a lie, that she looks absolutely radiant? In that case, wouldn't it be more loving to lift her up? Maybe not the perfect example, but you get my point (for the record, my wife's butt is amazing). So, is it possible that defining sin is not as simple as saying "thou shalt not" do this or that? Should our approach sound more like this: "Is this loving?" And should our conclusions about the scriptural legalities of a specific action be dependent on love rather than a list? Only you can decide for yourself, but approaching this book from the perspective of love could change your life. I believe that loving God and loving others is what the whole Bible boils down to. If any passages we attempt to interpret disagree with this, then we are not interpreting the passage correctly, and it must be reexamined. We spend our time parsing words, trying to figure out what they meant 2000 years ago. All in order to figure out if we are living and believing correctly. We then use that information to dictate our actions. We don't need to do that anymore. Jesus, John, and Paul have made it clear. If you love the one true God and love each other, you are living according to and fulfilling the "law." The law as it was given in the Old Testament has been replaced, as Jesus Christ is our new covenant. Hebrews 8:7 states, "For if that first covenant had been faultless, there would have been no occasion to look for a second." Verse 13 goes on to say, "In speaking of a new covenant, He (*Christ*) makes the first one obsolete. And what is becoming obsolete and growing old is ready to vanish away."

# Sexual Immorality

Deep breaths. Take several deep breaths. This is a good time for a reminder. Jesus Christ has already won. We can discuss and disagree on interpretations and opinions all day long, but we will be okay if we remember what really matters. In 1865, a widowed woman sat in the choir during a service at her church in Maryland. She wrote a poem on the fly-leaf of her hymnal, which would later become part of the hymnal itself:

> *And when before the throne*
> *I stand in Him complete,*
> *"Jesus died my soul to save,"*
> *My lips shall still repeat.*
> *Jesus paid it all, all to Him I owe;*
> *Sin had left a crimson stain,*
> *He washed it white as snow.*
> *(Jesus Paid It All, Elvina M. Hall)*

The next few chapters of this book will test you deeply. Everything you have been taught about sexual immorality, homosexuality, marriage, etc., will be under attack. And that's not a bad thing. When I began my studies a few years ago, the conflicting emotions I had were hard to bear. I was angry, confused, relieved, and thankful. Up until a few years ago, I would get angry when I heard someone defend homosexuality (a subject that requires its own section). I was disappointed by the sinful people who would visit a nude beach, have sex before marriage, have multiple sex partners, etc. I knew the scriptures. I knew what they taught, and it was "clear," a word thrown around by evangelicals who "clearly" don't know its meaning. In previous chapters, I have talked about how the Bible may not be inerrant, but I do believe it is inspired by God and useful for teaching. I also talked about how we are under a new law, the law of love, which should save us time parsing words and arguing over doctrine. However, in these next few chapters, I will be relying heavily on scripture, and I will be diving deep into the original words, their meanings, and the context behind passages. Why? Because that is the language of the Southern Baptist Church. If the law of love is not enough, perhaps some research and scriptural exposition will help.

In my research, I delved deep into both sides of whatever issue I was studying. I wanted to hear the arguments of both sides. Those of you into politics know what I am talking about. If you watch a conservative news station and never watch anything else, you may not be getting all the information needed for a balanced perspective. The same is true if all you watch is a liberal news station. Each side approaches the news with a certain degree of bias, which affects the way the news is presented, as well as the takeaway that forms the opinions of the broadcaster. I have found that by watching the news shows on both stations, I have better information, and I am able to better sift through the bias to get closer to the facts.

In studying sexual immorality, a few things seemed to stand out. The side of the Southern Baptist Church tended to rely mostly on the English translations of passages. They also used the phrase "scripture is clear" often. The opposing side tended to dive more into culture, context, and word meaning to arrive at their interpretation (perhaps because the issues hit closer to home for them). More often than not, the opposition's final opinion was recognized as just that, an opinion, and not something that scripture made crystal clear. This was extremely surprising to me because for most issues, the Southern Baptists are amazingly devout when it comes to scriptural exegesis. Exegesis is a fancy word that describes using culture, context, word meaning, and studies of the author and audience to arrive at a passage's meaning. I got a degree from an evangelical college, and exegesis was taught religiously, pun intended. After noticing the lack of contextual study on the subject of sex by evangelicals, I came to an eye-opening realization. I thought back on my time at Criswell College and realized that while we beat the scripture to death with context, translation, etc., not once did we ever broach the topics of sexual immorality, homosexuality, marriage, or the role of women in church and family. Fast forward 20 years, and I reached a turning point. That was the moment I started to question if what I had been taught at church as fact my whole life was the truth or not. Why did my school avoid these topics, and why did the church only give them a cursory glance? Was the church afraid of the ramifications of being wrong after hundreds of years of teaching one thing? Why was it that every time sexual issues were taught at church, they kept it at the surface level, using the English translated words to "clearly" define a belief? It then became my mission to research the tough topics.

The subject of sexual immorality in the Bible hinges mostly on twelve words, two Hebrew, and ten Greek. This does not include the study of homosexuality, which we will get to in a later section. Of those twelve words, two are only used once (*epithymetes* and *ekporneuo*), and one is used three times (*komos*). When you realize that some of the words are simply variations with the same base, the words are broken down into the following:

1. Lust/Covet/Desire (Hebrew: *Hamad, Ava*)

2. Lust/Covet/Desire (Greek: *epithymeo, epithymetes, epithymia*)

3. Sexual Immorality/Fornication (Greek: *ekporneuo, porneia, porneuo, porne, pornos*)

4. Sensuality (Greek: *aselgeia)*

5. Orgies (Greek : *komos)*

The Greek words *komos* and *aselgeia* are translated as "orgies" and "sensuality" by the English Standard Version (the Bible my church uses). These are the simplest words to address, so before we get into the rest, let's start there.

## Komos and Aselgeia

The following passages contain the word *komos:*

> *Let us walk properly, as in the daytime, not in* **orgies** *(komos) and drunkenness, not in sexual immorality and* **sensuality** *(aselgeia), not in quarreling and jealousy.* Romans 13:13 (ESV)

> *Now the works of the flesh are evident: sexual immorality, impurity,* **sensuality** *(aselgeia), idolatry, sorcery, enmity, strife, jealousy, fits of anger, rivalries, dissensions, divisions, envy, drunkenness,* **orgies** *(komos), and things like these.* Galatians 5:19-21a (ESV)

> *For the time that is past suffices for doing what the Gentiles want to do, living in* **sensuality** *(aselgeia), passions, drunkenness,* **orgies** *(komos), drinking parties, and lawless idolatry.* 1 Peter 4:3 (ESV)

The first thing you'll notice in these verses is the commonality of the lists of vices. They seem to all be referencing actions that are out of control. However, "sensuality" and "sexual immorality" (which we will discuss later) seem to not always require a lack of control. So, why does sensuality make the list? The Greek word here is *aselgeia* and is defined as an "unbridled lust, licentiousness, lasciviousness, wantonness, outrageousness." Vine's Expository Dictionary states that the best understanding of *aselgeia* is "Shameless conduct", or "that which is an insolent disregard for decency." When you look at the definitions of these English words, what you have is someone acting in a rude, disrespectful manner, that is indecent and obscene, lacking restraint and self-control. This can pertain to a sexual situation but does not always. For example, running through the streets naked, yelling and screaming while people are trying to sleep would certainly qualify as the word *aselgeia*. The English word "sensual" is not the best translation in this case, as you can be sensual and still be respectful and in control.

Back to *komos*, when we hear the English word "orgy," we automatically assume a group of people naked, having sex together. However, the word *komos* had a very different meaning at the time these passages were written. Vine's Expository Dictionary defines *komos* as "a revel, carousal, rioting." According to Blue Letter Bible (BLB), the way *komos* is used in scripture describes a common occurrence at the time:

> *a nocturnal and riotous procession of half drunken and frolicsome fellows who after supper parade through the streets with torches and music in honor of Bacchus or some other deity, and sing and play before houses of male and female friends; hence used generally of feasts and drinking parties that are protracted till late at night and indulge in revelry*

Suddenly, these three passages take on a new meaning, don't they? How did the translators of the English Standard Version arrive at the word "orgies"? Well, the word "orgy" has multiple meanings in English, one of which, according to Merriam-Webster, is:

> *secret ceremonial rites held in honor of an ancient Greek or Roman deity and usually characterized by ecstatic singing and dancing*

The dictionary goes on to give an example: "Roman orgies in honor of Bacchus." Sound familiar? That's the same definition we received from the Blue Letter Bible. The second definition from Merriam-Webster is the one we all assume when we read the word "orgy," which is a "sexual encounter involving many people." While technically correct in their use of the word "orgies," the translators of the English Standard Version (which came out in 2001) chose to use a word that most English speakers naturally associate with group sex. Here are a few other translations of Romans 13:13. My notes in brackets.

> *Let us behave decently, as in the daytime, not in carousing* [drinking alcohol and being noisy] *and drunkenness, not in sexual immorality and debauchery, not in dissension and jealousy. Romans 13:13 (NIV)*
>
> *Let us walk honestly, as in the day; not in rioting and drunkenness, not in chambering and wantonness, not in strife and envying. Romans 13:13 (KJV)*
>
> *Let us walk decently as in the day, not in reveling and drunkenness, not in illicit sex and licentiousness, not in quarreling and jealousy. Romans 13:13 (NRSVue)*

If you're a smart person, and I know you are, then you can see how different translations into our common language of English can take on very different meanings. Each of these translations was completed by large groups of Biblical scholars, yet one of them "clearly" missed the mark in its use of the word "orgies" by not considering the cultural meaning of that English word today. Relying solely on whichever English translation we choose to use is a misguided way of understanding what authors intended to communicate over 2000 years ago. And that is precisely why the church claims that only the original manuscripts of scripture are inerrant. We only have errant copies and translations in existence today, and as you can see, attempting to properly interpret them can get messy.

## Hamad and Ava

To properly understand the context of the Greek words we use to define "sexual immorality" and "fornication", we first need to understand the Hebrew words that we associate with lust, covet, and desire. There are two main Hebrew words that are translated into English as covet: *hamad* and *ava*. They are also translated into the following English words: lust, desire, crave, long for, delight, precious, greatly loved, and tasty, etc. The two Hebrew words are very closely related and considered interchangeable. In fact, there are two mentions of the Ten Commandments in scripture, one in Exodus and the other in Deuteronomy. In the tenth commandment, covet is mentioned twice. In Exodus, the word *hamad* is used both times. In Deuteronomy, *hamad* is used once and *ava* is used once. Both words can have either a good or bad connotation. It depends on the context in which they are used. The words are rarely translated as "lust"; however, some translations, such as the KJV, do use them that way. The KJV translates *ava* as "lust" five times in the Old Testament, all of them dealing with desiring meat or drink to consume, never in a sexual situation. The KJV translates *hamad* as "lust" once (Proverbs 6:25), dealing with the desire to take another man's wife from him (adultery). The ESV translates *hamad* in Proverbs 6 as "desire." The main reason for the difference in translations here is similar to the word "orgy" that we discussed earlier. The English word "lust" has more than one meaning. While the common definition that we think of today is "a very strong sexual desire," the second meaning is "a strong desire for something." Notice the second definition has nothing to do with sex, and that is the definition being used in the KJV.

The words *hamad* and *ava* did not carry a sexual implication. They are both used 28 times each in the Old Testament, for a total of 56 times. Only three of those usages can be remotely applied to sexual activity. All three deal with coveting your neighbor's wife. When *hamad* and *ava* are used with a negative connotation, it usually precedes the taking of something, or theft. For example, we see this in the tenth commandment:

> *You shall not **covet** (hamad) your neighbor's house; you shall not **covet** (hamad) your neighbor's wife, or his male servant, or his female servant, or his ox, or his donkey, or anything that is your neighbor's. Exodus 20:17 (ESV)*

This law, as the Jewish people understood it, taught that you are not to desire to take what your neighbor owns for yourself without consent. The neighbor, of course, was a man because women did not own anything. They were considered property of the man. And there were consequences for breaking this commandment. However, similar to the law in today's society, the consequences varied based on how grievous the crime was.

- The penalty for taking a man's ox was to pay back 5 heads of cattle to the man you stole from (Exodus 22:1)

- The penalty for taking a man's sheep was to pay back 4 sheep (Exodus 22:1)

- The penalty for taking a man's servant was death (Exodus 21:16)

- The penalty for taking a man's wife (adultery) was death (Leviticus 20:10) (Deuteronomy 22:22-24)

## Sexual Immorality in the Old Testament

As mentioned previously in this book, the New Testament authors only had the Old Testament at the time they lived and wrote. When they speak of something being "unlawful", the law they are referring to is the law of God as given in the Old Testament. New Testament scripture teaches that the old law no longer applies. John, Paul, and Jesus himself taught that the law can be boiled down to loving God and loving others. However, when speaking and teaching, Jesus and his disciples often referred to Jewish law, which was what their audience understood. Sexual immorality in the Old Testament was not a general, all-encompassing concept like it is today. Laws at that time were very specific, and the Jewish people were responsible for obeying them as written. All 613 of them, to be precise. In other words, instead of saying, "Don't be sexually immoral," it would be more specific, such as "Do not commit adultery," or "Do not covet your neighbor's wife." We have already discussed and determined that adultery, in every single example in the Old Testament, involved a married or betrothed woman. We also discussed why adultery was considered a bad thing (bloodlines, pure lineage, and theft of property). In fact, if you look through the list of 613 laws as

interpreted by Jewish Rabbis in today's society, the commandments regarding adultery say "do not covet or crave what belongs
to another" and are not specific to sex with another man's wife.
Proverbs 6:23-35 shows us just how important it was to not take
another man's wife from him. It also shows us that other sexual
relations done outside of marriage, such as sleeping with a prostitute, were not considered adultery.

> *For the commandment is a lamp and the teaching a
> light, and the reproofs of discipline are the way of life, to
> preserve you from the evil woman, from the smooth tongue of
> the adulteress.* Do not **desire (hamad, same word used in
> Exodus 20:17, tenth commandment)** *her beauty in your
> heart, and do not let her capture you with her eyelashes; for
> the price of a prostitute is only a loaf of bread, but a married
> woman hunts down a precious life. Can a man carry fire
> next to his chest and his clothes not be burned? Or can one
> walk on hot coals and his feet not be scorched? So is he who
> goes in to his neighbor's wife; none who touches her will go
> unpunished. People do not despise a thief if he steals to satisfy
> his appetite when he is hungry, but if he is caught, he will
> pay sevenfold; he will give all the goods of his house. He who
> commits adultery lacks sense; he who does it destroys himself.
> He will get wounds and dishonor, and his disgrace will not
> be wiped away. For jealousy makes a man furious, and he
> will not spare when he takes revenge. He will accept no com-
> pensation; he will refuse though you multiply gifts. (ESV)*

Wives were under the complete authority of their husbands,
considered not just property, but a special kind of property. They

were seen as the means through which a man continued his lineage. His impact on the world was at stake when someone potentially polluted the tool through which his bloodline was passed. In the Old Testament, a wife saw it as her duty to provide male offspring for her husband. It was so important that if she were unable to do so, she might provide an alternative solution. For example, Jacob (Israel), the father of the twelve tribes of Israel, had two wives (Leah and Rachel). Both of his wives, when unable to bear him children, gave Jacob their servants for him to sleep with. This was not considered adultery because the servants were not married to another man, nor was it against Jewish law. Sexual immorality in Old Testament times was based on adherence to very specific laws. Here are the Jewish laws regarding sex (paraphrased):

- If you don't like your wife, and divorce her, and she gets remarried, but then her new husband either dies or divorces her too, then you can't remarry her. (Deuteronomy 24:1-4)

- Jewish men and women were forbidden from being cult prostitutes. (Deuteronomy 23:17)

- If your brother dies without a son, it is your responsibility to take his wife and give her a son. (Deuteronomy 25:5, and yes, this was even if you were already married)

- If you have sex with a girl of marrying age who is not married or betrothed, you have to pay her father the bride-price. (Exodus 22:16)

- Don't have sex with animals. (Exodus 22:19)

- Don't have sex with your father's wife. (Deuteronomy 22:30)

- Don't have sex with close relatives (Leviticus 18:6)
- Don't have sex with your sister, granddaughter, aunt, daughter-in-law, brother's wife (while he's still living), sister-in-law, (Leviticus 18:9-18)
- Don't marry both a woman and her daughter (Leviticus 18:17)
- Don't marry both a woman and her granddaughter (Leviticus 18:17)
- Don't have sex with a woman during her menstrual period (Leviticus 18:19)
- Don't lie with a male as with a woman (likely referring to pagan ritual prostitution, more on this later; Leviticus 18:22)
- Don't have sex with your neighbor's wife (Leviticus 18:20)
- Don't marry gentiles (Deuteronomy 7:3)
- A priest can only marry a virgin of his own people (Leviticus 21:13)
- If a man has an emission of semen, he needs to take a bath, and he'll be unclean until evening. (Leviticus 15:16)
- A king must not have too many wives, horses, silver or gold (Deuteronomy 17:16-17)
- Do not have sex with a defeated enemy captive for one month to allow her to mourn first. If after you have sex with her you're not satisfied, you can let her go free. (Deuteronomy 21:11-14)

They can be boiled down into this list:

1. Don't be a cult prostitute.

2. Don't have sex with close relatives, animals, married women, women on their period, certain outsiders, or captive women (for one month).

3. If you have more than one wife, make sure they're not closely related to each other.

4. And if you have a wet dream, take a bath.

Men had multiple wives and concubines. This was okay because it was not against the law. In fact, we know God approved of the practice because He actually gave Saul's women to David (2 Samuel 12:8). People had sex outside of marriage. This was okay as long as it was done according to the law. We know this due to men using concubines, and the only mention of the loss of virginity in a negative way was concerning cult prostitution by the woman (Deuteronomy 22:21), which was against the law. We also know from Song of Solomon 2:3 that the couple participated in oral sex prior to marriage. The bottom line is: If it wasn't against the law, it was not immoral. Coveting (the same word as "lusting") was against the law when it included a strong desire to take what belongs to your neighbor without consent. And it is with that knowledge that we move into the New Testament Greek words that we define as "lust" and "covet."

# Epithymeo, Epithymetes, and Epithymia

As we discussed, the words *hamad* and *ava* were not used in a sexual sense in the Old Testament, except when describing the desire to take (steal) another man's wife. When the Old Testament was translated into Greek (the Septuagint, the bible the disciples used), the words *hamad* and *ava* were translated using the Greek words *epithymeo, epithymetes, and epithymia* (or some form of them).

- *Epithymeo* is used 34 times in the Septuagint, and 16 times in the New Testament. It is translated in the ESV as "to long for, to covet, and to desire." It is used in both a good and bad sense, depending on the context, but *epithymeo* is only used once to describe a sexual desire, in Matthew 5:28, regarding the theft of another's wife (adultery).

- *Epithymetes* is used 3 times in the Septuagint, and 1 time in the New Testament. It is translated in the ESV as "desire", and translated as "lust" and "crave" in the KJV and NASB (1 Corinthians 10:6). *Epithymetes* is used in a general sense and not used to describe a strictly sexual desire.

- *Epithymia* is used 40 times in the Septuagint, and 38 times in the New Testament. It is translated in the ESV as "desire, lust, passion, and covet." It is used in both a good and bad sense, but mostly bad. In the Septuagint, only one usage of *epithymia* describes a sexual desire, and it concerns desiring a married woman (Proverbs 6:25). In the New Testament, *epithymia* is used 7 times when listing general "desires of the flesh" (Colossians 3:5, Romans 1:24, Romans 13:14, Galatians 5:16, Ephesians 2:3, 2

Peter 2:18, and 1 John 2:16). In the Colossians, Romans and Galatians passages, there is an accompanying list of vices. These lusts of the flesh are described by Vine's Expository Dictionary as "not necessarily base and immoral, but are evil if inconsistent with the will of God."

The KJV translates *epithymeo, epithymetes, and epithymia* as "lust" 35 times in the New Testament. The ESV uses "lust" as a translation 3 times (Romans 1:24, 1 Thessalonians 4:5, and 2 Peter 2:10). The NASB uses "lust" 21 times, while the NIV uses "lust" 6 times. So, what is lust? Lust has two different meanings in the English language today. The first and main definition is "usually intense or unbridled sexual desire" (Mirriam-Webster), "a very strong sexual desire" (Cambridge), or "intense, uncontrolled, or illicit sexual desire or appetite" (dictionary.com). The second, less used definition is "an intense longing", "a powerful feeling of wanting something", or "to have a yearning or desire." The first definition is what the average American thinks of when they hear the word "lust." It has a very strong connection to sex. However, in the New Testament, of the 55 usages of the words *epithymeo, epithymetes, and epithymia*, only one has a direct connection to sex:

> You have heard that it was said, 'You shall not commit adultery.' But I say to you that everyone who looks at a woman with lustful intent (epithymeo, desire to take) has already committed adultery with her in his heart. (Matthew 5:27-28 ESV)

The words translated "*lustful intent*" come from the Greek word *epithymeo*. The addition of *epithymeo* (translated "lustful intent" here) shows the intention to steal. As discussed earlier, adultery is the taking of another's property without that person's consent. For example, if my neighbor has a one of a kind lawn mower, and I look at that lawn mower with the desire to take it from him and make it my own, that would be wrong. However, if I tell him how much I admire it and he permits me to borrow it, then no theft (adultery) would have been committed. I realize that is an extreme example, however it clarifies the difference between a desire to steal and a feeling of admiration. Jesus is stating that you should not look at another man's wife with the desire to steal her from him. Simply the desire in this case, even without taking action, is considered theft (adultery). It is hard in today's society to understand what Jesus was saying because women are no longer considered property of men. Today, admiring another person is not wrong. However, admiring a married person with the intent to have a sexual interaction with them without the consent of the other spouse, is wrong and considered cheating. It violates God's law of love. It's all about consent and intent.

Let's take a look at "lusts of the flesh", which is referenced 7 times in the NT with the word *epithymia*. (Bold has been added by me)

> *Put to death therefore what is earthly in you: sexual immorality* **(cult prostitution, more on this later)**, *impurity* **(moral uncleanness or lavish living)**, *passionate desire* **(pathos)**, *evil desire, and covetousness, which is idolatry.* *(Colossians 3:5)*

This passage is all about wanting more than you have and idolatry. The evil desire to take what doesn't belong to you and live a life of luxury. In essence, making idols out of material things. Not only is it unloving toward your neighbor, but it is unloving toward God as well, as he is having to compete for your love. It is idolatry. And with that understanding, we look at the next passage.

> *Therefore God gave them up in the lusts* **(desires)** *of their hearts to impurity* **(moral uncleanness or lavish living)**, *to the dishonoring of their bodies among themselves, because they exchanged the truth about God for a lie and worshiped and served the creature rather than the Creator.* *(Romans 1:24-25)*

This passage addresses the cultic idol worship rituals that were rampant at the time it was written. Cultic prostitution was a real problem, unlawful, and fundamentally unloving toward God. Due to their worship of idols, the people were treating their own bodies with contempt. Romans 1:26-32 further explains what these idol worshipers were doing during their rituals, and we will address those later in the section on homosexuality.

> *But I say, walk by the Spirit, and you will not gratify the desires of the flesh* **(natural tendency towards things evil)**. *For the desires of the flesh* **(natural tendency towards things evil)** *are against the Spirit, and the desires of the Spirit are against the flesh, for these are opposed to each other, to keep you from doing the things you want to do. But if you are led by the Spirit, you are not under the law. Now the works of the flesh are evident: sexual immorality* **(cult prostitution, more on this later)**, *impurity* **(moral**

*uncleanness or lavish living), sensuality **(shameless conduct, aselgeia)**, idolatry, sorcery, enmity, strife, jealousy, fits of anger, rivalries, dissensions, divisions, envy, drunkenness, orgies **(ceremonies honoring a false god, komos)**, and things like these. I warn you, as I warned you before, that those who do such things will not inherit the kingdom of God. (Galatians 5:16-21)*

Vine's Expository Dictionary defines "desires of the flesh" as "a phrase which describes the emotions of the soul, the natural tendency towards things evil. Such 'lusts' are not necessarily base and immoral; they may be refined in character, but are evil if inconsistent with the will of God." Any act done in the performance of idolatry is inconsistent with the will of God, because His will is for you to worship Him alone. This passage from Galatians warns against a list of evil actions, all of which are unloving toward our neighbors or unloving toward God. If we simply read the English translation, we can assume this passage is warning against lusting for the flesh (sex), having sex outside marriage, and the pursuit of sexual pleasure, including group sex. However, when we understand what the author (Paul) intended to convey in this letter, we see a very different picture. He is condemning unloving, evil actions. He goes on to contrast those actions with what is good. Let's read the rest of this section of his letter to see if our new understanding makes sense now:

*But the fruit of the Spirit is love, joy, peace, patience, kindness, goodness, faithfulness, gentleness, self-control; against such things there is no law. And those who belong to Christ Jesus have crucified the flesh **(the earthly nature of*** *humanity, Greek word "sarx") with its passions and desires. If we live by the Spirit, let us also keep in step with the Spirit. Let us not become conceited, provoking one another, envying one another. (Galatians 5:22-26 ESV)*

These actions are in direct contrast to the evil actions he had just previously described. Read each one separately and see that it is a direct contrast to evil. If sexual immorality (in our modern understanding of that phrase) is what was being condemned, then a consensual sexual relationship outside marriage would be a contrast to love, joy, peace, kindness, and gentleness. That simply does not make sense. Now that we have translated this passage correctly, we can interpret it to mean: "Don't be unloving and out of control. Be loving and in control."

2 Peter 2 is a chapter all about false prophets and teachers. This passage specifically addresses the way in which these false prophets draw people in by appealing to their desire for earthly things. Sounds familiar, doesn't it, with so many preachers today teaching a gospel of prosperity and material wealth.

*For, speaking loud boasts of folly, they entice by sensual **(shameless, aselgeia)** passions **(desires, epithymia)** of the flesh **(the earthly nature of humanity, sarx)** those who are barely escaping from those who live in error. (2 Peter 2:18)*

The final two passages relating to the desires of the flesh (Ephesians 2:3, and 1 John 2:16) summarize what we have learned in the passages above. Read them through your new lens:

*And you were dead in the trespasses and sins in which you once walked, following the course of this world, following the prince of the power of the air, the spirit that is now at work in the sons of disobedience—among whom we all once lived in the passions of our flesh, carrying out the desires of the flesh and the mind, and were by nature children of wrath, like the rest of mankind. But God, being rich in mercy, because of the great love with which he loved us, even when we were dead in our trespasses, made us alive together with Christ—by grace you have been saved (Ephesians 2:1-5)*

*Do not love the world or the things in the world. If anyone loves the world, the love of the Father is not in him. For all that is in the world—the desires of the flesh and the desires of the eyes and pride in possessions—is not from the Father but is from the world. And the world is passing away along with its desires, but whoever does the will of God abides forever. (1 John 2:15-17)*

We now know how to properly interpret the words lust, covet, and desire. God does not want us to live our lives wanting more, or desiring what belongs to someone else. He also does not want us to live in an out-of-control manner. We need to stay far away from idolatry, which could involve the direct worship of a false god, or the love of material possessions. Idolatry is un-loving toward God. Once again, through research and proper interpretation, we find ourselves arriving at a familiar concept: Love God, and love others.

## Sexual Immorality in the New Testament

*Ekporneuo, Porneia, Porneuo, Porne and Pornos.* Ok, let's get this out of the way first. Yes, the word *pornography* comes from these Greek words. And no, they don't refer to sexually stimulating visual aids. Also, the word *sandwich* does not refer to a sorceress that lives on the beach. The interpretation of these Greek words by the early church fathers has been one of the most damaging mistakes in the history of Biblical interpretation. Add to that our lack of understanding of the culture of early Christians under Roman rule, and you have the perfect recipe for a Southern Baptist youth group conference on saving sex for marriage. I attended one of these weekend retreats at our local Baptist encampment with my childhood church in Dallas, Texas. I was middle school age, and I still remember the scene vividly. I was sitting in a room full of boys listening to a man talk about how he hadn't masturbated in three years. I was told that all sexual contact of any kind was wrong before marriage. My youth leaders affirmed the following list of sinful acts:

- Masturbation
- Oral sex
- Intercourse
- Sex outside of marriage
- Looking at a sexy lady with more than a cursory glance
- Looking twice after a cursory glance
- Simply thinking about sex
- Viewing pornography
- Using sex toys

We were told that if we committed these sins, we were going against the will of God. The two-day study culminated in a request for everyone to sign a "commitment card." This card was a vow to family, friends, future mate, and future children, to remain sexually pure until a marriage partner is found and a covenant has been formed. One by one, every single child at the conference signed the commitment cards. It was more out of peer pressure than true commitment. Unfortunately, this peer pressure was coming from the adults. Looking back on the situation, I find myself wondering what the adults were thinking. They left no room for questioning or deep discussion. They simply pounded a few verses down the throats of the children, many of whom were pre-pubescent. Then they instructed the kids to sign a card promising they would believe and abide by it until they were married. I signed the card.

My commitment was genuine, but it didn't last long. That same year (8th grade), I attended a party with some school friends. They decided to play spin-the-bottle. Initially, I was hesitant, but I eventually gave in to the peer pressure. It felt naughty, but I kissed several of the girls. They were just pecks during the game, but later that evening, my friends dared a girl and me to french kiss. We went out on the back porch, and she laid it on me hot and heavy. It was wet and messy, and it felt really good. I liked it a lot, actually. But I quickly felt the shame that came with knowing I had sinned. I felt shameful because the parents and youth leaders had told me this was wrong. It's sexual immorality, right? Lust? Isn't it wrong to enjoy the physical pleasure of touching and being touched by someone else? I had let God down… again…and again. The shame and guilt that I felt were very real.

Over time, I became heavily involved in our church in various capacities. I started working for the youth and media departments as an intern while attending the Bible College associated with the church. One of my vivid memories was attending deacons' meetings. Providing media support, I was the only one in the room who was not a deacon or pastor. I witnessed the fighting that would break out over disagreements regarding the direction the church was going. The fighting was typically over trivial matters, and it left an awful taste in my mouth. Is this really what Jesus had in mind for the Church? My experiences as a staff member of the church really opened my eyes. If deacons could disagree on so many things, that meant that not all of them were right. What else could the church be wrong about? Up to that point, I had taken what I was taught in church as the gospel, so to speak. I blindly trusted what I was told and patterned my behavior to match. The irony of the whole situation is that during this same time, I was being taught at Bible College to question everything. It makes me angry to look back on that and know that the shame could have been avoided if the leaders in the Christian community had been more careful in their interpretation of scripture.

This teaching on purity stuck with me until I was 42 years old. My marriage was in a rut. We loved each other deeply, but with four kids and life, we didn't make much time for each other. My wife was quick to point out consistently that we hadn't been on a vacation together without the kids since our first child was born. Fifteen years of not connecting had taken a toll. We had sex and thoroughly enjoyed it when we did, but we were lucky to be intimate once a week, twice on a good week. Then I found a document online. It was a long checklist for Christian couples, written by an anonymous Christian author because the subject is still too taboo for the church. It listed an action or a verbal phrase, and then you placed a checkmark on a sliding scale of whether you are disgusted by it or really turned on by it. Some examples of what were listed:

- Sucking on my spouse's toes
- My spouse kissing my neck
- Dancing
- Shaving pubic hair
- Cuddling
- Having my spouse strip for me
- Cunnilingus
- A variety of sexual positions
- Having ejaculate swallowed
- Sexting
- Saying "naughty words" during sex (it was quite a list)
- Having sex in various places, like the forest, a hot tub, or the beach

It was 27 pages of things like this. I filled it out by myself, and my wife filled it out by herself. When we had completed it, we sat down together and compared notes to see what we had been missing in our sex life. One of the things that stood out was that we were both interested in having sex in different places. A forest sounded fun. Outside, surrounded by trees, with nobody around. So, with that in mind, we decided to take that vacation that we needed. Just the two of us. We booked a weekend trip to the Poconos in Pennsylvania. We stayed at one of those resorts where the rooms had a two-story champagne glass hot tub, a private indoor swimming pool, a private sauna, and a massage table. Oh, and the gift shop had a section with lube, massage oil, and… (*whispers*)….*sex toys*. Just outside our room was a hiking path that led into the woods. Without going into too much detail, let's just say we checked several things off our list that weekend.

Using the list, our communication improved by leaps and bounds. We got home from the "sexcation" and felt like newlyweds again. My wife asked me, "Hey, where do you want to go have sex next?" We both looked at each other, and I jokingly suggested we go get naked on a beach. We shared a little chuckle. However, that got me thinking. And when I start thinking, I start researching. I started looking for an Airbnb on a secluded beach. I found a few, but they were very expensive places to visit. I also found less expensive options, however, they were on nude beaches with other people around. We can't do that, can we? It's wrong to look at other people naked. What if I like what I see? Phrases that we read in scriptures, and that the church has always taught me, kept ringing through my head: *sexual immorality!!!* So, I started thinking again, which led to, you guessed it…researching. I googled and googled and googled. I got my Bible out, and my trusty dictionaries and commentaries, and I went to town. And it seemed every day my eyes were opened more and more. My wife thought I was crazy when I had my "Eureka!" moments. And those moments led to some very deep theological discussions between the two of us. I knew that I couldn't be silent about this. I couldn't let other children (including my own) grow up in evangelical churches today, only to suffer the same fate of shame and guilt. That's when I decided to write this book.

The reason I waited until this point in the book to tell this story is because the interpretation of *ekporneuo, porneia, porneuo, and porne* is what started my life-changing research. The term "sexual immorality" is very broad and vague. Who decides which actions to include when interpreting that phrase? Is it the same people who gave me the list at my youth retreat in 8th grade? If my church leaders thought it was important to give us a list of forbidden sexual acts, then why didn't the authors of the New Testament do the same? For example, masturbation is not mentioned in the Bible once. However, the church believes that thinking about sex (sexual fantasies) with someone other than your spouse is sexually immoral, and you commit this sin when you masturbate. *Got Questions* is a conservative, evangelical website that answers questions from a biblical perspective. This is what they have to say:

> *A sexual fantasy creates a sexual act or event in the imagination. Depending upon the nature of the fantasy and the imagined players in it, a sexual fantasy can be a sin. Any imagined scenario that is inappropriate for moral, ethical, or spiritual reasons is sinful. (https://www.gotquestions.org/sexual-fantasy.html)*

That is how the church justified telling me it was a sin. So, if masturbation is sin because it requires a sexual fantasy, then how do we know that sexual fantasy falls into this category of sexual immorality? Is it this verse?

*But I say to you that everyone who looks at a woman with lustful intent (epithymeo, covet, the intent or desire to take what belongs to another without their consent) has already committed adultery with her in his heart. (Matthew 5:28 ESV)*

Or this one (more on this verse later)?

*For out of the heart come evil thoughts, murder, adultery, sexual immorality, theft, false witness, slander. These are what defile a person. (Matthew 15:19-20 ESV)*

This verse seems to suggest that thinking about sex is evil and poisons you if you're not married. Ouch. I tried looking up the phrase "sexual immorality" in the dictionary, but it's not there. However, if you take the definitions of the two words separately and combine them, you get something like this: "a sexually motivated behavior that is outside society's standards of acceptability." So, it depends on society then. Which one? Thank God the Bible wasn't written in English in the 21st century. If it were, most of us would be in serious trouble. No, the Bible was written many thousands of years ago, over the course of more than 1500 years. The New Testament, from which we derive our understanding of "sexual immorality," was written almost 2000 years ago. Morally acceptable behavior can vary based on different societies within the same time period. For example, going topless or even nude at a public beach in France is normal, but try that in Galveston and watch the parents rush to shield their childrens' eyes. How much more can morally acceptable behaviors vary when societies are not just separated by geography, but also by 2000 years? Or is it possible that we've interpreted the Greek words *completely* wrong, and it's not about "sexual morality" at all? Every book in the New Testament was written by a Jewish author (with the possible exception of Luke, but that's a different conversation). However, the Jewish people at the time of Jesus were under Roman rule. Depending on where one lived, some areas were more immersed in Roman culture than others. The language mostly used at the time was Greek. So, like we've done with other words, the best way to find out what "sexual immorality" really meant when the authors penned it is to research the Greek words the authors used, and the culture at that time.

## Ekporneuo, Porneia, Porneuo, Porne and Pornos

Let's break these words down a little:

*Ekporneuo* is used 43 times in 37 verses in the Septuagint (Greek translation of the Old Testament, the Bible used by the disciples), and 1 time in the New Testament. It is translated in the New Testament ESV as "Sexual Immorality." BLB (Blue Letter Bible) translates it as "to go a whoring."

- *Porneia* is used 46 times in 39 verses in the Septuagint, and 25 times in the New Testament. It is translated in the ESV as "sexual immorality" all but one time, and that one is simply "immorality" but in a sexual context dealing with prostitution as a metaphor for Babylon, the chief seat of idolatry. (Revelation 19:2). BLB translates it as "unlawful sexual intercourse," or as a metaphor "the worship of idols."

- *Porneuo* is used 18 times in the Septuagint, and 8 times in the New Testament. It is translated in the ESV as "sexually immoral person", and "practice or commit sexual immorality." BLB translates it as "to prostitute one's body", and "to give one's self to unlawful sexual intercourse," or as a metaphor "to be given to idolatry, to worship idols."

- *Porne* is used 37 times in 35 verses in the Septuagint, and 12 times in the New Testament. It is translated in the ESV as "prostitute." BLB translates it as "a woman who sells her body for sexual uses," or as a metaphor "an idolatress."

- *Pornos* is used 0 times in the Septuagint, and 10 times in the New Testament. It is translated in the ESV as "sexually immoral person, the sexually immoral." BLB translates it as "a male prostitute" or "a man who indulges in unlawful sexual intercourse."

Of the 37 verses containing *Ekporneuo* in the Septuagint, all but 3 directly reference idol worship or cult prostitution. The three remaining refer to prostitution, but it is unclear if it is cult prostitution as the context is ambiguous. Of the 39 verses containing *Porneia* in the Septuagint, every single one references idol worship or cult prostitution. Of the 18 verses containing *porneuo* in the Septuagint, every single one references idol worship or cult prostitution. Of the 35 verses containing *Porne* in the Septuagint, 16 of them reference idol worship or cult prostitution, 18 reference a female prostitute (with no indication if it was cult-related or not), and the remaining one verse references a forbidden woman (also translated as "adulteress").

So, what is the takeaway from the above Septuagint numbers? The Greek words *ekporneuo, porneia, porneuo, and porne* were used 129 times in the Septuagint, and *ALL BUT ONE* (that's 128 of 129) unambiguously refer to idolatry, prostitution, or a combination of the two. The one remaining verse speaks of an immoral woman, most likely an adulteress, which would be a married woman who wants to seduce a man that is not her husband (Proverbs 5:3).

The New Testament authors who used these Greek words when writing were quite familiar with the way they were used in ***their Bible*** (the Septuagint). In fact, when Paul, and all the other New Testament authors, quote Old Testament verses, they are often quoting directly from the Septuagint. When they read those words while reading their Bibles, they understood them to mean prostitution and idol worship (idol worship being false gods as well as "lusts of the flesh" like gold, silver, material possessions, and anything that takes your love away from God).

Why would they then use those same words when they wrote their books but change the meanings to be an all-encompassing ban on everything sexual outside of marriage? They wouldn't do that. As I write this book, I imagine how it would be received if I took the word "Christian" and changed the meaning to be an all-encompassing word that meant "anyone who believes in a higher power." If I want my readers to understand what I am saying, I need to speak their language. So when I say "Christian," I need to mean "believer in Jesus Christ as savior." The word Christian is more restrictive than simply someone who believes in God. It means something specific and is not a general term for a list of people.

In the same way, the Greek words *ekporneuo, porneia, porneuo, and porne* each have a specific meaning, and we just found out what that is: idolatry and prostitution (usually done as a form of idolatry). In fact, one of the books of the Apocrypha that did not make it into our evangelical Bible is the Book of Wisdom (also called Wisdom of Solomon). It is, however, in the Catholic Bible. Book of Wisdom 14:12 says, "*Porneia* began when idols were invented."

Now let's take that knowledge, combine it with what we have learned previously, and reinterpret some misunderstood passages.

Remember this one from a few pages ago?

> *For out of the heart come evil thoughts, murder, adultery, sexual immorality, theft, false witness, slander. These are what defile a person. (Matthew 15:19-20 ESV)*

For context, Jesus had just finished calling the Pharisees hypocrites. They had questioned why his disciples didn't wash their hands before eating, which was a tradition they followed. He sarcastically reminded them that they broke God's commandment (honoring your father and mother) for the sake of the tradition of washing hands. Then, he told them through an Old Testament quote that they shouldn't teach tradition as if it were doctrine (are we sure he wasn't talking to the Southern Baptist Church?). Well, that offended the Pharisees and seemed to confuse Peter as well, so Jesus explained that what comes out of the mouth proceeds from the heart, and he gave a list (*evil thoughts, murder, adultery, sexual immorality, theft, false witness, slander*).

Now, keep in mind that the first four of the 10 commandments teach love for God, and the final six teach love for others.

Jesus had already mentioned honoring your father and mother (5th commandment). Now check this out: "Evil thoughts" (10th commandment), "murder" (6th commandment), "adultery" (7th commandment), "theft" (8th commandment), "false witness and slander" (9th commandment). Each word on the list Jesus gives is one of the Ten Commandments, except for one. Can you guess which one? Yep...*sexual immorality*. The commandments that are not represented in his list are the first four, the ones about loving God. If only we had a word for that. Enter the word that was used by the author: *porneia*. It was used throughout the Old Testament to describe *idolatry* and *turning one's love away from God*. Let's plug that into the verse and see if it makes more sense now (I've also added the rest of verse 20):

> *For out of the heart come evil thoughts, murder, adultery, porneia, theft, false witness, slander. These are what defile a person. But to eat with unwashed hands does not defile anyone. (Matthew 15:19-20 ESV)*

Jesus was speaking the language of the Pharisees, those men who constantly pestered the Jewish people about keeping the letter of the Mosaic Law but sometimes broke the law for the sake of tradition. Essentially, Jesus was saying, "Your traditions don't matter anymore. What matters is my commandments, and guess what? A few chapters later in the gospel of Matthew, I'm going to boil those 10 commandments down into two categories: Love God and love others."

Do you remember the time Esau sold his birthright?

*Once when Jacob was cooking stew, Esau came in from the field, and he was exhausted. And Esau said to Jacob, "Let me eat some of that red stew, for I am exhausted!" (Therefore his name was called Edom). Jacob said, "Sell me your birthright now." Esau said, "I am about to die; of what use is a birthright to me?" Jacob said, "Swear to me now." So he swore to him and sold his birthright to Jacob. Then Jacob gave Esau bread and lentil stew, and he ate and drank and rose and went his way. Thus Esau despised his birthright. (Genesis 25: 29-34 ESV)*

Paul recalls this story when writing Hebrews.

*...that no one is sexually immoral (pornos, male prostitute) or unholy like Esau, who sold his birthright for a single meal (Hebrews 12:16 ESV)*

If you read the passage from Genesis, it's hard to find anything sexual about what Esau did. If you try to interpret the Hebrews passage according to the English translation, you're going to be very confused. However, if you interpret it with your new understanding of *pornos (male prostitute)*, it makes perfect sense. Esau sold himself for food.

Paul uses the word *pornos* again in the next chapter of Hebrews:

*Let marriage be held in honor among all, and let the marriage bed be undefiled, for God will judge the sexually immoral (pornos) and adulterous. (Hebrews 13:4)*

During Roman rule, it was common for men to engage in what was called "pederasty." Look up that term. It's quite interesting. Pederasty was an accepted practice at the time Paul wrote Hebrews, and involved a grown man (usually married) and a young boy. The young boy was considered a prostitute or slave of the older man, and the man used the boy for his sexual pleasure. It was a very one-sided, non-consensual relationship. What Paul is referencing in Hebrews 13:4 is that you should be loving towards your spouse. The man should not cheat by having sex with boys (pederasty), and the woman should not cheat by committing adultery. We know that Paul's goal here was love because of the preceding verses:

> *Let brotherly love continue. Do not neglect to show hospitality to strangers, for thereby some have entertained angels unawares. Remember those who are in prison, as though in prison with them, and those who are mistreated, since you also are in the body. (Hebrews 13:1-3 ESV)*

In fact, all of Hebrews 13 is about love, whether it's love for God, or love for others. It's not the only time sexual immorality and adultery are used together. Listen to Jesus's words from his sermon on the mount in the gospel of Matthew:

> *It was also said, 'Whoever divorces (apolyo) his wife, let him give her a certificate of divorce (apostasion).' But I say to you that everyone who divorces his wife, except on the grounds of sexual immorality (porneia), makes her commit adultery, and whoever marries a divorced woman commits adultery. (Matthew 5:31-32 ESV)*

The word being translated in the ESV here as "divorce" is *apolyo*. It means "to send away." It's used 66 times in the New Testament, including when Jesus dismisses (sends away) the crowds or his disciples. It's also used when Pilate releases (sends away) Barabbas. The word translated as "certificate of divorce" means precisely that, a "bill of divorce." Divorce, at that time and even today, was not considered official until there was a certificate of divorce. Men would abandon their wives without a certificate, which left them, you guessed it, still married. This verse is saying that if you send away your wife without divorcing her (unless she has been prostituting herself out, *porneia*), then you make her commit adultery. Why? Because adultery is a married woman having sex with someone, and she is technically still married, because you sent her away without a certificate. Therefore, whoever marries that "sent away" woman now commits adultery too, because he is having sex with another man's wife. Understanding the words really helps.

*"All things are lawful for me," but not all things are helpful. "All things are lawful for me," but I will not be dominated by anything. "Food is meant for the stomach and the stomach for food"—and God will destroy both one and the other. The body is not meant for sexual immorality (porneia), but for the Lord, and the Lord for the body. And God raised the Lord and will also raise us up by his power. Do you not know that your bodies are members of Christ? Shall I then take the members of Christ and make them members of a prostitute? Never! Or do you not know that he who holds fast to a prostitute becomes one body with her?*

*For, as it is written, "The two will become one flesh." But he who is joined to the Lord becomes one spirit with him. Flee from sexual immorality (porneia). Every other sin a person commits is outside the body, but the sexually immoral person (porneuo) sins against his own body. Or do you not know that your body is a temple of the Holy Spirit within you, whom you have from God? You are not your own, for you were bought with a price. So glorify God in your body. (1 Corinthians 6:12-20 ESV)*

If you read this passage with the knowledge that porneia is idolatry and cult prostitution, it really takes on a whole new meaning. It's all about keeping God first. Don't replace Him with something else. Your body is God's temple. So why would you sin against your own body by worshiping a false god? Paul then goes directly into this passage:

*Now concerning the matters about which you wrote: "It is good for a man not to have sexual relations with a woman." But because of the temptation to sexual immorality (porneia), each man should have his own wife and each woman her own husband. (1 Corinthians 7:1-2 ESV)*

Paul starts by quoting something the church in Corinth wrote to him in a letter about it being good to not have a wife. That's something Paul agrees with, but he adds if you're tempted to get your sex from the temple prostitutes, don't do it. Get married instead. And he goes on to say the married couple shouldn't deprive each other of said sex.

Similar to the 1 Corinthians 6 passage, Paul wrote to the Thessalonians about the need to love God:

> *For this is the will of God, your sanctification: that you abstain from sexual immorality (porneia); that each one of you know how to control his own body in holiness and honor, not in the passion of lust (epithymia, **desire**) like the Gentiles who do not know God; that no one transgress (hyperbain) and wrong (pleonekteo) his brother in this matter, because the Lord is an avenger in all these things, as we told you beforehand and solemnly warned you. For God has not called us for impurity (akatharsia), but in holiness. (1 Thessalonians 4:3-7)*

The word translated as "impurity" is *akatharsia*, which means "physical or moral uncleanness" (also luxurious, lavish living) and does not have a sexual connotation. The word translated as "transgress" is *hyperbain*, which means "to step over." The word translated as "wrong" is *pleonekteo*, which means "to have more, or be superior to, take advantage of."

A few short years ago, I would have read this passage and thought it was teaching me to be sexually pure, not having sex outside of marriage (or masturbate, or enjoy the sight of a pretty lady, yada yada), because it's God's will that I control myself. That's the way this passage, and others like it, have always been presented in the Southern Baptist Church. Let's read it again, but with our new understanding. I am also adding what Paul says directly after in order to see the complete picture.

*Finally, then, brothers, we ask and urge you in the Lord Jesus, that as you received from us how you ought to walk and to please God, just as you are doing, that you do so more and more. For you know what instructions we gave you through the Lord Jesus. For this is the will of God, your sanctification: that you abstain from idolatry (porneia, or cult prostitution); that each one of you know how to control his own body in holiness and honor, not in cravings to want more (epithymia) like the Gentiles who do not know God; that no one steps over (hyperbain) and takes advantage (pleonekteo) of his brother in this matter, because the Lord is an avenger in all these things, as we told you beforehand and solemnly warned you. For God has not called us to be unclean, but to be holy. Therefore whoever disregards this, disregards not man but God, who gives his Holy Spirit to you.*

*Now concerning brotherly love you have no need for anyone to write to you, for you yourselves have been taught by God to love one another, for that indeed is what you are doing to all the brothers throughout Macedonia. But we urge you, brothers, to do this more and more, and to aspire to live quietly, and to mind your own affairs, and to work with your hands, as we instructed you, so that you may walk properly before outsiders and be dependent on no one.*

*(1 Thessalonians 4:1-12)*

Paul is reminding the people of what he taught them: the instructions of Jesus. And then he goes on to explain what those instructions were. The first section concerns itself with love for God, and the second section concerns itself with love for others.

That sounds familiar. It doesn't at all sound like the church teaches it. Another passage that the church uses regularly to condemn "sexual immorality" is found in 1 Corinthians 10:

> *Do not be idolaters as some of them were; as it is written,*
> *"The people sat down to eat and drink and rose up to play." We*
> *must not indulge in sexual immorality (porneuo, idolatry, cult*
> *prostitution) as some of them did, and twenty-three thousand*
> *fell in a single day. We must not put Christ to the test, as some of*
> *them did and were destroyed by serpents, nor grumble, as some*
> *of them did and were destroyed by the Destroyer. Now these*
> *things happened to them as an example, but they were written*
> *down for our instruction, on whom the end of the ages has come.*
> *Therefore let anyone who thinks that he stands take heed lest he*
> *fall. No temptation has overtaken you that is not common to*
> *man. God is faithful, and he will not let you be tempted beyond*
> *your ability, but with the temptation he will also provide the*
> *way of escape, that you may be able to endure it. Therefore,*
> *my beloved, flee from idolatry (eidololatria, means idolatry, the*
> *worship of false gods). (1 Corinthians 10:7-14 ESV)*

The church uses this verse to say that God will help you escape the temptation to lust after a person, or masturbate, or whatever sexual "sin" you want to include in "sexual immorality." However, this is actually one of the best passages that proves the true meaning of the variations of *porneia*. The whole passage is about idolatry. In fact, the ESV even has the subheading "warning against idolatry" above this passage. The English phrase "sexual immorality" is way out of place. If *porneuo* has any sexual connotation here, it is in the form of cult prostitution, which was idolatry.

There is one more passage I would like to discuss before moving on from *porneia*: **1 Corinthians 5**. The Corinthian church, as we can see from some of the passages we discussed above, had a problem. They were starting to turn to idol worship. They participated in the cultic rituals that were prevalent at that time in Corinth. You see, Corinth was known for its cult (or temple) prostitution. It has been well-documented in secular sources that it was the heart of cult prostitution in ancient Greece. The Greeks believed that the goddess of love, Aphrodite, was born there. According to the Greek philosopher and historian Strabo (64 BC to 24 AD), the temple for Aphrodite had upwards of 1,000 girls who worked as prostitutes there. About 450 years prior to the New Testament period, the Greek historian Herodotus wrote about the Babylonian women. In that culture, every woman was required, at least once in her life, to prostitute herself for money outside the temple. However, men were also known to sell themselves as temple prostitutes. This was the culture of the ancient Greek people. Paul had heard that the people of the church at Corinth were participating in cult prostitution (1 Corinthians 5:1, translated in ESV to "sexual immorality"). What made it even worse is that one of them participated in the ritual with his father's wife! That was one of the reasons he wrote the letter to the church there. In the letter, he reminds them that their bodies are a temple of God.

*Do you not know that you are God's temple and that God's Spirit dwells in you? If anyone destroys God's temple, God will destroy him. For God's temple is holy, and you are that temple. (1 Corinthians 3:16-17 ESV)*

God is a jealous God. This is recorded many times throughout scripture. God Himself even wrote it out on the ten commandment tablets:

> *You shall have no other gods before me. You shall not make for yourself a carved image, or any likeness of anything that is in heaven above, or that is in the earth beneath, or that is in the water under the earth. You shall not bow down to them or serve them, for **I the Lord your God am a jealous God**, visiting the iniquity of the fathers on the children to the third and the fourth generation of those who hate me, but showing steadfast love to thousands of those who love me and keep my commandments. (Exodus 20:3-6 ESV)*

God hates idolatry, and anything that takes the love of His creation away from Him. People had built temples to these false gods, and they were selling their bodies to worship them. Paul was reminding the Corinthians that as Christians, their *bodies* are God's temple. He resides within them via the Holy Spirit. By using their bodies to serve false gods, they were destroying God's temple.

This last section of the 1 Corinthians 5 passage is very important because it creates a link to our next topic. Unlike all of the other Corinthian passages we discussed previously, Paul chooses to use the word *pornos* here instead of *porneia*. He is directly addressing the fact that the men of the Corinthian church were selling themselves at the temple (most likely male-male sex). Keep in mind that the *type of sex* being had (male-male, male-female) in all of these Corinthian passages is not what is important. The message Paul is sending is to stop being unloving to God, destroying His temple (your body) by worshiping false gods, which is idolatry. The ESV translates *pornos* to "sexually immoral people," so I have corrected that:

> *I wrote to you in my letter not to associate with male prostitutes (pornos)—not at all meaning the male prostitutes (pornos) of this world, or the greedy and swindlers, or idolaters, since then you would need to go out of the world. But now I am writing to you not to associate with anyone who bears the name of brother if he is a male prostitute (pornos) or greedy, or is an idolater, reviler, drunkard, or swindler—not even to eat with such a one. For what have I to do with judging outsiders? Is it not those inside the church whom you are to judge? God judges those outside. "Purge the evil person from among you." (1 Corinthians 5:9-13 ESV, with edits of the word pornos)*

Men were serving as cult prostitutes in Corinth. And it is with that understanding that we discuss the issue of homosexuality.

## Homosexuality

There are six main passages that the church points to when condemning homosexuality. There are three in the Old Testament, and three in the New Testament.

- Genesis 19:4-5
- Leviticus 18:22
- Leviticus 20:13
- 1 Timothy 1:9-10

- 1 Corinthians 6:9-10

- Romans 1:26-27

Since the New Testament is fresh in our minds, let's start there. Paul begins his letter to Timothy by explaining why Timothy should stay in Ephesus. Paul instructs him to teach people there to NOT focus on doctrines that deviate from the truth. He says they should stay focused on the things of God, which is by *faith*. He specifies that the goal of their teaching is *love* that comes from a *pure heart,* a *good conscience,* and a *sincere faith.* Paul goes on to say that certain people have swerved from love and have wandered away into fruitless discussions. He says those people want to be teachers of the law, but they don't understand what they're saying, even though they are confident in their beliefs.

I couldn't think of a more appropriate introduction to the next two verses. The evangelical church has confidently maintained over hundreds of years that loving, consensual homosexual relationships are sinful. I believe the intentions of the church have been good; however, their understanding and interpretation of scripture have been wrong. We discussed sexual immorality in the previous chapter and discovered that it wasn't sexual immorality at all. It was idolatry. Idolatry in every form, whether it be sexual (as a worship ritual for a false god), material (in the form of money and possessions), or of the heart (a deep desire to have more). It is with that new knowledge that we read this passage from 1 Timothy:

> *Now we know that the law is good, if one uses it lawful-*
> *ly, understanding this, that the law is not laid down for the*
> *just but for the lawless and disobedient, for the ungodly and*
> *sinners, for the unholy and profane, for those who strike their*

*fathers and mothers, for murderers, the sexually immoral (pornos), men who practice homosexuality (arsenokoites), enslavers, liars, perjurers, and whatever else is contrary to sound doctrine. (1 Timothy 1:8-10 ESV)*

The English phrase here, "the sexually immoral, men who practice homosexuality," has been translated directly from the use of two Greek words. Commas did not exist in the ancient Greek language, so English translators are making an assumption when they divide these two phrases. The phrase as written by Paul sounds like this: "pornos arsenokoites." We know that *pornos* means a male prostitute, likely in connection with cult prostitution as Paul used it this way before in 1 Corinthians. But what does *arsenokoites* mean? This one is extremely difficult to figure out. It is a word that Paul made up and is only used twice in the whole New Testament, both times by Paul. It is a compound word made up of two Greek words that are found in the Septuagint: *Arren* (which means "male" or "male child") and *koite* (which means "bed" or "sexual intercourse"). Vine's Expository Dictionary defines it as "abuser." Other possible definitions include:

- Abuser of one's self with mankind (BLB)
- One who lies with a male as with a female (BLB)
- Male-bedder
- Male who has sex
- Male abuser
- Sex with male child

Based on the context of the list Paul is giving, it's safe to assume that whatever it means, it's not a good thing. I believe Vine's is onto something with "abuser". It could possibly be "abuser of a male child". Regardless, the fact is we simply don't know exactly what he meant. However, when you pair the word with *pornos*, as Paul did, you get a better picture of what he is referring to. Together, *pornos arsenokoites* becomes "male prostitute abuser" or something similar. This could refer to pederasty (discussed previously), which was a master/slave, man/boy sexual relationship that was common at the time. Or, it could refer to male cultic prostitution between two men. If you separate the two words as our ESV does, then Paul could possibly be referring to both pederasty *and* cult prostitution between men. Either way, this does not sound like a loving homosexual relationship, and certainly does not sound like the "sound doctrine" of which Paul speaks. He already told us exactly what that sound doctrine is:

> *The aim of our charge is love that issues from a pure heart and a good conscience and a sincere faith. (1 Timothy 1:5 ESV)*

Remember our passage from 1 Corinthians 5, where Paul condemned the men of the church for engaging in cultic prostitution? Well, this next passage is what he said immediately after. In 1 Corinthians 6:1-8, Paul really lays into the people of the church. They were suing each other in court rather than settling matters on their own or through the church. He very animatedly tells them how stupid that was. He then says:

> *But you yourselves wrong and defraud—even your own brothers! Or do you not know that the unrighteous will not*

*inherit the kingdom of God? Do not be deceived: neither the sexually immoral (pornos, male prostitutes), nor idolaters, nor adulterers, nor men who practice homosexuality (arsenokoites), nor thieves, nor the greedy, nor drunkards, nor revilers, nor swindlers will inherit the kingdom of God. And such were some of you. (1 Corinthians 6:8-11a ESV)*

This is a direct reference to what Paul had just discussed with them in chapter 5. And there's that pesky word again, *arsenokoites*. This time, the two words *pornos* and *arsenokoites* are clearly separated. This time *arsenokoites* could be a reference to pederasty, or it could be the "male abuser" of the male prostitute. Regardless, it is most likely referring to some sort of abuse, and is, again, a direct reference to what he said in chapter 5. He then spends the rest of chapter 6 talking about cult prostitution and the need to love God with your body, which is His temple (discussed previously). Context and culture are everything in understanding this new word.

Paul first visited Corinth around 50 AD, then he wrote a letter to them that was lost. A few years later, after hearing of their idolatry, he wrote the 1 Corinthians letter. Soon after he wrote the letter, he visited again, which in his words was a "painful visit." The Corinthian church was not changing its ways. He then wrote another letter, delivered by Titus, which we don't have. Titus told Paul the church responded well to that letter, however they still questioned Paul's authority. That prompted him to write another letter (2 Corinthians), and soon after that he visited Corinth again. It was during this final visit that Paul wrote the letter to the Romans while staying with Gaius (who helped found the Corinthian church). Paul had been engrossed in the issues plaguing the Corinthians, namely cult prostitution. So, now we have set the scene. Paul had cult prostitution on his mind, and he was staying at the house of one of the leaders of the church with the problem. He starts the letter by introducing himself, followed by letting the Romans know how badly he wants to go to Rome. He then goes directly into a discussion on idolatry and the wrath of God that comes as a result. He talks about how the ungodly and unrighteous will incur the wrath of God. He says they "exchanged the glory of the immortal God for images resembling mortal man and birds and animals and creeping things" (Romans 1:23 ESV). As a result, those unrighteous men "dishonored their bodies." "They exchanged the truth about God for a lie and worshiped and served the creature rather than the Creator" (Romans 1:24-25). I believe he is talking about the Corinthians here. He continues:

> For this reason God gave them up to dishonorable passions. For their women exchanged natural relations for those that are contrary to nature; and the men likewise gave up natural relations with women and were consumed with passion for one another, men committing shameless acts with men and receiving in themselves the due penalty for their error. (Romans 1:26-27 ESV)

Given the context of the passage, we know that this relates to idol worship, in particular cult prostitution. How do we know this? Because he says "For this reason" directly after saying they dishonored their bodies, worshiping the creature rather than the creator. Also, remember, he was sitting in Corinth…staying with a Corinthian… dealing with the Corinthians. I could stop right there and be perfectly content knowing that this verse does not refer to a loving, same-sex relationship. However, there are a couple of things to note that help us better understand this passage. The use of the words "nature" and "natural" here are the Greek words *physis* and *physikos*. They are translated correctly here. However, the way Paul uses the word suggests an interpretation more along the lines of "culturally acceptable." Take, for example, his use of the same word in 1 Corinthians 11:14: "Does not nature itself teach you that if a man wears long hair it is a disgrace for him?" He was saying that men know naturally not to have long hair. I wouldn't say that comes naturally to men in today's society. Perhaps what comes "naturally" is dependent on the culture you are in. It comes naturally for a man to not gawk at a topless sunbather in France. However, it's not so easy for a man who's not used to that sort of thing. The disciple Peter also uses the word in 2 Peter 2:12 and the ESV translates it as "instinctual." If we read the Romans passage from that standpoint, we could possibly come to the conclusion that anal sex is what was being discussed. The women had anal sex, and "likewise" the men did too. Maybe, like growing long hair, that was taboo at the time. When Paul talked about the long hair, he said it was a disgrace. The word he used (*atimia*) is the same one that is translated "dishonorable" in Romans.

The bottom line here is that we don't know for certain what sex acts are being performed in these verses, but we DO know it was being done in the setting of cult prostitution and in an unloving way. This passage is NOT condemning *loving* acts that come *naturally* to people in the 21st century United States of America. And no, the Bible does not say you can't have long hair. It was perfectly acceptable in Samson's culture.

When discussing Old Testament laws, we need to remember that as Christians, we are no longer under the old law. Our instructions are clear: to love God and love our neighbors. So, it pains me to study an Old Testament law in order to attempt to apply it to how we are expected to live today. The church believes that since "homosexuality" is brought up by Paul, then the old law still applies. Oops. I guess they haven't read my book yet. The New Testament does not condemn what we see in today's culture, which is loving, consensual same-sex relationships. Therefore, there is no reason to believe those Old Testament laws apply today, even if they *were* outlawing that sort of behavior. If we believe we are still under those laws, then here is a list of other things that should still apply today:

- No eating pig (goodbye pulled pork sandwiches)
- No eating shellfish (goodbye shrimp and crab)
- No tattoos
- No trimming the corners of your beard
- No wearing clothes made with two materials
- Women can't wear men's clothes
- And don't get me started on all the rules about sacrifices

That being said, I want this subject to be thoroughly covered, so let's take a look at these Old Testament passages and see what we've got. During the time of Abraham (pre-Old Testament law), there were a couple of cities called Sodom & Gomorrah. They are famous for being destroyed by God due to their evil actions. Abraham's nephew, Lot, lived in Sodom, but he was the only innocent one there. We don't know many specifics about these evil sins, but we do know they were grievous enough for Jesus himself to come check out the situation with two angels. In Genesis 18, we see three men walking toward Sodom, and they pass by the area where Abraham was camped out. Abraham recognizes them as Jesus (the Lord) and two angels and begs them to come stay with him for a while. Abraham and Sarah pamper them with food and treat them very well. Eventually, they got up to continue going toward Sodom. Abraham walked with them to see them out. As they were walking, the Lord asked the two angels if he should tell Abraham what he's about to do to Sodom. He continues to say that the outcry has been so bad that he needs to see if it's as bad as he has heard. At that point, the two angels turned away and went toward Sodom. Abraham pleads with the Lord to spare Sodom. They went back and forth for a while, and the Lord agreed to spare Sodom and Gomorrah if he found at least ten righteous people there. The Lord then left, and Abraham went home. The two angels arrived at Sodom in the evening, and Lot (Abraham's nephew) saw them because he was standing near the entrance to the city. He bowed down in front of them and invited them to his house to spend the night. They initially declined and said they would sleep somewhere in the town square, but Lot insisted, and they agreed. That night, all of the men in Sodom surrounded Lot's house and demanded that he bring the two men out so they could rape them. Lot pleaded with them not to do it and offered them his two daughters instead, to do with as they pleased. The crowd insisted that Lot give them the two men and moved to storm the house. At that time, the two angels intervened, pulled Lot back inside, and struck the crowd with blindness so they couldn't find the door. The angels then instructed Lot to flee Sodom and take his family with him because they were going to destroy the city. Once they had fled, God destroyed Sodom and Gomorrah.

The church uses this passage to condemn homosexuality. Many claim that the reason God came to destroy them was that their males were having sex with other males. But is that really the reason the cities were destroyed? To find out more about the sins of Sodom, we look toward a few passages outside Genesis. In Matthew 10, we see Jesus giving instructions to his disciples. He is sending them into the surrounding Jewish towns to tell others about Him. He tells them that if anyone doesn't welcome them, they will be worse than Sodom and Gomorrah:

> *And if anyone will not receive you or listen to your words, shake off the dust from your feet when you leave that house or town. Truly, I say to you, it will be more bearable on the day of judgment for the land of Sodom and Gomorrah than for that town. (Matthew 10:14-15 ESV)*

Here we see Jesus comparing the behavior of these people with Sodom. What was so bad about their behavior? They were unkind and rejected the message of the disciples. In essence, they rejected God.

Next, we go to Ezekiel 16. Here we find the Lord comparing Jerusalem with Sodom. God describes having blessed Jerusalem's people greatly. However, in response, they have turned their backs on Him. God describes them as having played the whore:

> *But you trusted in your beauty and played the whore (zana) because of your renown and lavished your whorings on any passerby; your beauty became his. You took some of your garments and made for yourself colorful shrines, and*

*on them played the whore (zana). The like has never been, nor ever shall be. You also took your beautiful jewels of my gold and of my silver, which I had given you, and made for yourself images of men, and with them played the whore. (Ezekiel 16:15-17 ESV)*

The word translated as "whore" in the ESV is the Hebrew word *zana*, which means "to commit adultery", "to be a cult prostitute", "to be unfaithful to", or "to be a harlot." Based on the context of this passage, I believe it may mean all of those put together. Israel (the bride of God) was *unfaithful* to God, cheating on Him by worshiping false gods (*adultery*). She gave her beauty to any passerby (*harlot*), playing the whore while worshiping idols (*cult prostitution*). At the core, what God is upset about is that Jerusalem (Israel, God's people) had rejected Him, turning their love toward false gods. But God wasn't done describing Jerusalem just yet. He kept going, and going, and going, about their whoredom and unfaithfulness toward Him. Israel had completely and totally rejected God through idolatry. God's bride had been unfaithful. God then makes the comparison of what Israel had done with Sodom, telling them that they were worse than Sodom:

*Not only did you walk in their ways and do according to their abominations; within a very little time you were more corrupt than they in all your ways. As I live, declares the Lord God, your sister Sodom and her daughters have not done as you and your daughters have done. **Behold, this was the guilt of your sister Sodom: she and her daughters had pride, excess of food, and prosperous ease, but did not aid the poor and needy. They were haughty and***

***did an abomination before me.*** *So I removed them, when I saw it. (Ezekiel 16:47-50)*

Next, we're going to check out the "book" of Jude. Jude was an apostle and a relative of Jesus, either a brother or cousin depending on who you ask. He wrote a very small portion of scripture. The epistle of Jude has only one chapter and is quite short. The whole of Jude is a warning about false teachers. He was referring to a specific group of people, but we don't know exactly who they were. He described them in the following ways:

- Ungodly (*asebes,* meaning without reverential awe toward God)

- They pervert the grace of God into wantonness (lack of control)

- They reject Jesus Christ

- They defile the flesh

- They reject authority

- They blaspheme (speak evil of) the glorious ones (*doxa,* a thing or creation belonging to God, an angel)

Wait, they blaspheme the angels? What does that mean, exactly? Well, take a moment and read through Jude. You will find that the group Jude is referring to, these false teachers, were really perverting the message of Christ. They spoke evil things about the things of God. Jude writes:

> *But these people blaspheme all that they do not understand, and they are destroyed by all that they, like unreasoning animals, understand instinctively. (Jude 1:10 ESV)*

Remember that word "natural" from Romans 1:26-27 (*physikos*)? That is what is translated here as *instinctively*. Jude is saying that these false teachers don't understand the things of God (which can also be interpreted as "angels"). By instinct (what comes naturally to them), the false teachers don't understand the things of God and therefore treat them poorly. Let's expand this passage a bit and see the verses before it:

> *Now I want to remind you, although you once fully knew it, that Jesus, who saved a people out of the land of Egypt, afterward destroyed those who did not believe. And the angels who did not stay within their own position of authority, but left their proper dwelling, he has kept in eternal chains under gloomy darkness until the judgment of the great day—just as Sodom and Gomorrah and the surrounding cities, which likewise indulged in sexual immorality (ekporneuo) and pursued unnatural desire (eteros sarx), serve as an example by undergoing a punishment of eternal fire. Yet in like manner these people (the false teachers Jude speaks of) also, relying on their dreams, defile the flesh, reject authority, and blaspheme the glorious ones. But when the archangel Michael, contending with the devil, was disputing about the body of Moses, he did not presume to pronounce a blasphemous judgment, but said, "The Lord rebuke you." But these people (false teachers) blaspheme all that they do not understand, and they are destroyed by all that they, like unreasoning animals, understand instinctively. (Jude 1:5-10)*

Jude is making a comparison between the *things of God, angels,* and *humanity* here. They are all three equally of God, and to treat them unlovingly is to treat God unlovingly. The angels Jude speaks of, who left their own position of authority, are referring to angels that left their position in heaven and committed some evil deed. This is most likely referring to the angels in Genesis 6. The earth was becoming populated, the angels saw that the women were beautiful, and they had sex with them, resulting in children. Their offspring were called the Nephilim, who were giant, mighty men. Enoch, the great-grandfather of Noah, wrote about this in 1 Enoch, and part of his writing is quoted in Jude 1:9, where it talks about the archangel Michael. After the angels had committed this act, God saw that the wickedness on earth was out of control, and He decided to destroy it with a flood. The passage in Jude above compares what these angels did with earthly women to the sins of Sodom and Gomorrah. Because Sodom and Gomorrah "*likewise indulged in sexual immorality (ekporneuo) and pursued unnatural desire (eteros sarx)."* This is the only time in the New Testament that the word *ekporneuo* is used. We know from its use in the Septuagint that it means "idol worship," "cult prostitution," or "prostitution" in general. The phrase *eteros sarx* means "strange flesh" or "flesh of a different nature." This most likely refers to the angels in Sodom, who were of a different nature, similar to the angels in Genesis 6. So we take what we have learned here, and we can interpret this passage to mean: *The people of Sodom treated the angels with evil intentions, wanting to violate them sexually just like the angels likewise did with the people of earth. In like manner, these false teachers defile the flesh, reject authority, and speak evil of things belonging to God.*

The sin of Sodom was not a loving, consensual same-sex relationship. The sin of Sodom was the rejection of God through their evil behavior. Their list of evil deeds was extensive, and one thing on the list was the desire to gang rape angels. While the church associates Sodom with homosexuality, it does so mistakenly.

That leaves two verses in the Old Testament that the church uses to condemn homosexuality. They are both Mosaic laws: Leviticus 18:22 and Leviticus 20:13. The only real difference between the two is the addition of the death penalty in Leviticus 20:13.

> *You shall not lie with a male as with a woman; it is an abomination. (Leviticus 18:22 ESV)*

> *If a man lies with a male as with a woman, both of them have committed an abomination; they shall surely be put to death; their blood is upon them. (Leviticus 20:13 ESV)*

This law against a man lying with a man was punishable by death. Of the 613 laws, about 36 carried the death penalty. The Mosaic laws were first recorded in Leviticus and then reiterated in Deuteronomy. In fact, the word *Deuteronomy* means "copy or repetition of the law." Of all the laws in Leviticus that prescribe the death penalty, all of them are listed in Deuteronomy. Well, all but ONE. You guessed it: a male lying with a male. However, a new law does appear in Deuteronomy:

> *None of the daughters of Israel shall be a cult prostitute, and none of the sons of Israel shall be a cult prostitute. (Deuteronomy 23:17 ESV)*

Do we really need to keep discussing this? I think it's clear throughout scripture that cult prostitution was not only a reality but also something that God detested because it took love away from Him.

We now know (from our studies of 1 Corinthians and 1 Timothy) that the New Testament scriptures condemning "homosexuality" were, in actuality, condemning cult prostitution and idolatry. And we see that Leviticus was likely doing the same. So why should we hang our hats on Old Testament law to condemn homosexuals today? If we do so, shouldn't we condemn other Old Testament laws as well, such as having sex with a woman during her period, charging interest on loans, eating pork, or getting tattoos? Christ explained that the Sabbath was made for man, not the other way around (Mark 2:27). The law was created to maintain order for the Israelites, who had a hard time remembering how to honor and glorify their creator and treat each other with kindness. That was the purpose of the law, and Jesus confirmed this when he rephrased the original intention of the law: to love God and love others.

In today's culture, wearing long hair for a man comes *naturally* for some and not for others. Similarly, attraction to members of the same sex comes *naturally* for some and not for others. The vast majority (95-96%) of Americans are naturally attracted to members of the opposite sex. That is why it is so difficult for us to understand that attraction to members of the same sex comes naturally to others. But like those false teachers in Jude, we don't understand the things of God. Scripture does not condemn loving, consensual same-sex relationships. And neither should we.

# Marriage

Marriage is one man, one woman, together for life. This is what I have always been taught, always believed, and until the last few years, never questioned. The evangelical church, generally speaking, has always taught that the creation of Adam and Eve is a blueprint for marriage. It is God's divine plan for humanity. Let's look at some examples. Krista Bontrager, of *The Theology Mom* podcast, states in part 3 of her 4-part homosexuality series "Is It a Sin to be Gay?":

> *"The consistent thread throughout the canon of scripture is that God's ideal definition of marriage consists of one man, and one woman, becoming one flesh, for one lifetime."*

In discussing Romans 1:26-27, Bontrager states:

> *"Homosexuality is a creation issue. It is an origins issue. All roads lead us back to Genesis. If you just look at creation, and look at how God had set things up, you can kinda know how they work."*

Glenn Stanton, of Focus on the Family, in the book titled *My Crazy Imperfect Christian Family: Living Out Your Faith with Those Who Know You Best*, states the following:

> *"In Genesis, God declares His purpose for Adam and Eve, that they unite together in marriage and "be fruitful and multiply (Genesis 1:28)."*
>
> *"God designed this marriage union to be permanent, committed, exclusive and self-giving. It is a complete union—emotional, spiritual and physical—with the possibility of producing new life (Genesis 2:23-24)."*
>
> *"Any kind of sexual sin—whether sex outside of marriage, pornography, homosexuality, rape, lust or fantasy—all falls short of God's design of the union of a husband and wife."*
>
> *"The story begins with God creating humanity in His image, male and female. Two distinct but complementary creatures, made for each other. Together, man and woman were fashioned to reflect the image and likeness of God. Male and female, together, are the fullest picture of the image of God in creation. That's why they need each other."*

The following is an excerpt from the beliefs section on the website of my church:

> *We believe that marriage is a union ordained by God and intended as a lifelong commitment between one man and one woman. (Genesis 1:27-28, Genesis 2:18, Matthew 19:4-9, Mark 10:5-9, Ephesians 5:31-33). In keeping with the Bible's clear teaching on marriage as being between*

*one man and one woman — Elders, Ministry staff, or any*
*member ordained by the church will not conduct same-sex*
*wedding ceremonies. Moreover, facilities will solely be used*
*for marriage ceremonies between a man and a woman.*

Other Southern Baptist churches, and most evangelical
churches, say something similar. The church clearly believes that
God's design for marriage is presented in the creation story in
Genesis, and nothing other than that design is permitted. If, as
the church believes, the divine plan of God for marriage is one
man and one woman together for life, then I have some questions that need to be answered.

- Why did God allow Adam to search for a possible companion among the animals prior to creating Eve?

- If Adam and Eve were the first "marriage" then who made
  up the second marriage?

- Can God's divine plan change?

- Why did God allow, and approve of, men having multiple wives?

- If the image of God is only realized with both a man and
  a woman, together, then why does Paul recommend not
  getting married?

- Did Jesus define marriage in Matthew 19?

Before we delve into answering these questions, let's examine
the passages in Genesis where we encounter the concept of marriage as "God's design." There are two creation stories depicted
in Genesis. One narrates the day-by-day creation of the world
(Genesis 1:1-2:3), which some believe to be literal days while

others interpret it figuratively. The second creation story is more focused on the creation of humans. (Genesis 2:4-25)

*Then God said, "Let us make man in our image, after our likeness. And let them have dominion over the fish of the sea and over the birds of the heavens and over the livestock and over all the earth and over every creeping thing that creeps on the earth." So God created man in his own image, in the image of God he created him; male and female he created them. And God blessed them. And God said to them, "Be fruitful and multiply and fill the earth and subdue it, and have dominion over the fish of the sea and over the birds of the heavens and over every living thing that moves on the earth." (Genesis 1:26-28)*

*So the Lord God caused a deep sleep to fall upon the man, and while he slept took one of his ribs and closed up its place with flesh. And the rib that the Lord God had taken from the man he made into a woman and brought her to the man. Then the man said, "This at last is bone of my bones and flesh of my flesh; she shall be called Woman, because she was taken out of Man." Therefore a man shall leave his father and his mother and hold fast to his wife, and they shall become one flesh. (Genesis 2:21-24)*

In the first creation account, plants were created on day three, and then God created Adam and Eve together on day 6. However, in the second creation account, the plants have not grown yet due to a lack of someone to work the land. The plants didn't grow until after Adam was created, and long before Eve was created. I say "long before" because of the numerous events that transpired between Adam and Eve in the second account. It states that God created Adam, and then God planted the Garden of Eden, and then He made the trees spring up, and then he made the rivers flow through it. And I know what you're thinking. God could do all of that in the snap of a finger. That is true, but then he saw that it wasn't good for Adam to be alone. And he gave him the task of naming all the animals and determining if any of them would be suitable for a mate. Now, God may not be restricted by time, but Adam sure was. Surely the amount of time it would take for Adam to go through all the animals one by one would be longer than a literal day. In any case, after Adam went through the animals, he didn't find a suitable helper. Now, this word "helper" is used by many to imply she was more like a servant, subservient. However, the Hebrew word used here is *ezer*, and it means "helper" but in more of a partnership sense. Equal partners. We know this because of the way it is used throughout the rest of the Old Testament. The same word is used to describe God when he helps people out (Exodus 18:4 for example). God is certainly not subservient. Since Adam couldn't find a partner to his liking, God put him under anesthesia, took one of his ribs, and built Eve out of that rib. When Adam saw Eve, he knew right away that she was one of his kind ("bone of my bones, flesh of my flesh"), and he named her "ishshah" *(woman)* because she was taken out of "ish" *(man)*. And the next verse says:

> *Therefore a man shall leave his father and his mother and hold fast to his wife, and they shall become one flesh. (Genesis 2:24 ESV)*

In today's culture, it is the woman who leaves her father, not the man. The man is expected to carry on his father's name. Traditionally, the woman takes on the last name of her husband and leaves her father. That's why we always ask, "Who gives this bride away?" And a hesitant father stands up and reluctantly says, "I do." Does this mean we have it backwards? I'm just bringing up that point to be silly, but do you remember this 1 Corinthians passage we studied earlier? Paul quotes directly from Genesis 2:24:

> *Or do you not know that he who is joined to a prostitute becomes one body with her? For, as it is written, "The two will become one flesh." But he who is joined to the Lord becomes one spirit with him. (1 Corinthians 6:16-17)*

Paul is using Genesis 2:24's "become one flesh" phrase to describe a purely physical encounter with a cult prostitute. There is no emotional bond there. It doesn't imply they are now to be together for life. If he understood "become one flesh" to mean a lifetime commitment, then why did he use it this way? The Hebrew word translated as "flesh" in Genesis is *basar*, which refers to the physical body. It indicates they become one physically, and we know that because Paul then contrasts that with being joined to God, which is oneness in spirit, not body. The reality is, we don't precisely know what Genesis 2:24 means, but it is probably not "one man, one woman, for life." Because if this were a full, complete description of what God's divine plan for marriage is supposed to look like for everyone, then it only contradicts itself as soon as two chapters later in Genesis 4:19 ("Lamech took two wives"). What we ***know*** from all these Genesis passages is:

- We were made in his image
- He created two types of us
- It's not good for us to be alone
- Adam and Eve were told to populate the earth

All we have are these Genesis verses and a couple of examples of people quoting Genesis 2:24 ("become one flesh") in a different context without defining marriage (more on this later). And with that, I'm going to attempt to answer my own questions from above.

## Animal Companions

Did God really allow Adam to search among the animals for a companion before creating Eve? I don't want to waste much space answering that question because the truth is we can never know the answer to that for sure. If He did, then He may have been trying to point out the uniqueness of Eve. Perhaps the author of the second creation account was trying to emphasize how Eve was the perfect companion for Adam. Or maybe God was simply making the point that it's possible to be attracted to many types. Regardless, I don't think Adam really had the option of choosing an antelope for his companion. However, the subject of animals in creation brings up an interesting question that does require some thought: How did God create *nature* to behave?

*For his invisible attributes, namely, his eternal power and divine nature, have been clearly perceived, ever since the creation of the world, in the things that have been made. (Romans 1:20)*

Is the one male/one female dynamic something that applies across the board, or just to humans? We know marriage was not a legal matter because the law wasn't around yet. And when the law came about, the only laws regarding marriage failed to define it. In fact, some of them regulated having more than one wife. So prior to the law, how did people know what God expected of them? We know from scripture that God expected people to love Him (not worship false Gods) and to be hospitable (love each other). We know this from stories like Sodom and Gomorrah, the fall in the garden, etc. But as for specifics beyond that, people just did what came *naturally*. Now, human cultures and behaviors tend to change dramatically over time. We know this because they change dramatically just by hopping on an airplane. And we love to make up rules for how to live. But what can we learn from animals? Animals live instinctively, by *nature*. They do what comes *naturally*. What kinds of relationships did God create in the *natural* world?

According to the National Science Foundation, only 3-5% of the over 4,000 mammal species practice any form of monogamy. Additionally, many species of animals exhibit same-gender sexual activity, as well as companionship. For instance, 1 in 10 rams (male sheep) mate only with other rams. Amazon dolphins and garter snakes engage in group sex. Several animals, like clownfish and green frogs, are hermaphrodites (they can change their sex). Banana slugs and copperhead snakes can impregnate themselves without a mate. The sex of sea turtles is determined by the temperature where the eggs are laid.

Let's consider the black swans for a moment. Twenty-five percent of all black swan pairings are homosexual in nature. They are also monogamous. They let females build a nest and lay eggs, then the two males will run the female off and raise the young together. But did God create creatures that way from the beginning? Logic would say no. If God created two male black swans, then they would be the last black swans in existence. When God created creatures, He created them with the ability to procreate, to "be fruitful and multiply."

> *And God blessed them, saying, "Be fruitful and multiply and fill the waters in the seas, and let birds multiply on the earth." (Genesis 1:22 ESV)*

However, He also created them with instincts that lend themselves to companionships of all kinds, whether emotional, sexual, or both. The *natural* animal world contains lots of interesting relationships and behaviors, and those animals were all created by God. But they weren't created in His image. Humans were:

> *Then God said, "Let us make man (adam, mankind) in our image, after our likeness. (Genesis 1:26 ESV)*

God's image is what separates us from the other animals. The difference between animals and humanity is the ability to reason (like I'm doing now). We think logically to determine the difference between right and wrong. Reason is why we search for happiness beyond God. Reason is why we go against our *nature* and rebel against our creator. Animals don't have that, so they rely on the *natural* instincts that God gave them. They don't decide right and wrong. They don't question God and worship idols. They behave the way God created them to behave, *naturally*. And to them, relationships of all kinds come *naturally*. They have no choice in the matter because they can't reason. So you see, when God blessed and told Adam and Eve to "be fruitful and multiply" (just like He did the animals) in Genesis 1:28, we shouldn't assume that meant only male-female relationships are in God's divine plan for humanity forever. However, they're definitely both needed to procreate. Ask me how I know.

## The Second Marriage and God's Divine Plan

- In the ESV, the word "marriage" only appears twice in Genesis. It does not appear again until after the law was written.

- The word "married" only appears once in Exodus (Ex 21:3), and doesn't appear again until after the law was written.

In Genesis, both passages employ the same Hebrew word, which we translate as "marriage." The word is *issa* ("woman, wife, female"), which is the same word Adam used to name his companion "woman" (he didn't name her Eve until later on). In both verses (Genesis 38:14 and 41:45), the woman is being given by someone to a man. In Exodus, two Hebrew words are being translated as "married." They are *ba'al* ("owner, husband, lord, or ruler) and *issa* ("woman, wife, female"). ESV translates this as "married," but given what we know about the culture of that time, what the author was literally saying was more akin to "the owner of the woman." In actuality, the concept of marriage as we know it today did not exist during the whole of the Old Testament times. Women were viewed as property, and divorce happened regularly. Women could not own anything. When they were divorced, they were forced to be homeless or become a prostitute. This is why Jesus would later address divorce as something men shouldn't do unless the wives were unfaithful (Matthew 5 and 19). It was unloving toward the woman. Back then, people did not hear or read the story of creation and think, "Ok, one man, one woman, one lifetime." And their understanding of "marriage" continued for thousands of years. So why do we, who are living thousands of years later, think we can interpret the creation of humans more clearly than those who lived just after we were created? What knowledge do we have that they didn't have?

Some argue that the fall and the entrance of sin are the reasons God's design was corrupted. For the sake of argument, let's assume that's true and that Adam and Eve indeed were the picture of God's divine plan for marriage. If so, then who would have been the man and woman to compose the second marriage if Adam and Eve had never taken a bite of that fruit? There would have been no sin, therefore no corruption of God's design. Adam and Eve were already taken, their vows presided over by God Himself. The next marriage would have been between the son and daughter of Adam and Eve. There's no other option unless Adam and Eve were not literal people, which would present a whole slew of new problems (we're not going there in this book). So, now we know that incest was originally part of God's divine plan. Adam and Eve could not have carried out the command to "be fruitful and multiply" without it. There's no getting around that. If one assumes that the Genesis account describes God's divine plan for marriage, then one must also believe that incestual marriage is part of that divine plan. Otherwise, the divine plan only applied to Adam and Eve and nobody else. If one maintains that incestual marriage wasn't wrong until later on when the law was introduced, then one must also admit that God's divine plan changed. If God's divine plan changed, then it was not permanent. That kind of throws a wrench in Krista Bontrager's theory:

> *"Homosexuality is a creation issue. It is an origins issue. All roads lead us back to Genesis. If you just look at creation, and look at how God had set things up, you can kinda know how they work." (The Theology Mom, Is It a Sin to be Gay?)*

One of my favorite movies is *The Princess Bride*. In it, one of the characters, Vizzini, continues to use the word "inconceivable" over and over. You may be picturing the scene in your head right now. Eventually, Inigo Montoya says to him, "You keep using that word. I do not think it means what you think it means" (I bet you read that in his accent). In the same way, how God "set things up" is not what we think it is.

## The P Words (Polygamy & Patriarchy)

When Adam & Eve betrayed God, it came with consequences. The serpent lost its legs, and men had to work harder until they returned to the earth (death). For women, childbirth became painful and, while they desired the man, the man would rule over the woman.

> *I will surely multiply your pain in childbearing; in pain you shall bring forth children. Your desire shall be contrary to your husband, but he shall rule over you. (Genesis 3:16 ESV)*

What does this mean, exactly? I don't know. Most translations say "your desire will be for your husband," and the ESV has that in its footnotes, so why the ESV translators decided to translate it "contrary" is beyond me. The Hebrew word used here is "*el*," and it means both "toward" and "against" (also "concerning" or "on account of") depending on context. So maybe it's just signifying some sort of conflict between spouses. The word translated as "rule" is "*Masal*" and means "rule, reign, or power." Regardless, we simply need to look at nature to answer why patriarchy was an issue. Men are physically strong. There are exceptions, of course, but we can't deny that overall, the muscle structure of men is stronger than women. Maybe it was the way we were created. Maybe it was a result of the fall. We don't know. It just is. But men can also be *pretty stupid* (3,000 years from now, people will translate that as *good looking idiots*). We solve arguments with fistfights and wars. We tend to use our biceps rather than our brains. So, it is no wonder that men decided we would be in charge. As I write this, I can almost hear the historians, philosophers, and theologians critiquing me. However, I believe it really is that simple. Men are strong, stupid, and arrogant. And that causes problems. One of those problems was (and is) the imbalance and inequality between men and women. Perhaps that is how we should be reading Genesis 3:16. The woman's desire will be "concerning" the man (she'll want to help since she's smart and has a good intuition) but he will overpower her. We will never know the details of how it came about exactly, but males became the rulers of humanity. Love is the purpose of life, but sin is the poison that corrupted it. We were created equal. As discussed before, woman was created from the side of man, as an equal partner and helper. But she became property, something to be owned. She was owned by her father until he sold her to another man. And if a man could afford it, he could own more than one. When he became tired of her, he could send her away. Even by the time of Jesus, women were still being divorced for any and every reason. That's what led the Pharisees to ask Jesus this question:

> *And Pharisees came up to him and tested him by asking,* *"Is it lawful to divorce one's wife for any cause?" He answered,* *"Have you not read that he who created them from the be-* *ginning made them male and female, and said, 'Therefore a* *man shall leave his father and his mother and hold fast to his* *wife (gyne,), and the two shall become one flesh'? So they are* *no longer two but one flesh. What therefore God has joined* *together, let not man separate." (Matthew 19:3)*

The church uses this passage to assert that Jesus was defining marriage, but he was not. The Greek word translated as "wife" here is *gyne* and means "a woman of any age, whether a virgin, married, or a widow" (BLB). Vine's Expository Dictionary defines *gyne* as "a woman, married or unmarried." Additionally, remember that Paul used the term "become one flesh" to describe an impermanent sexual encounter with a prostitute (1 Corinthians 6:16-17). Furthermore, we must consider Jesus's audience, the Jewish Pharisees. They did not interpret the Genesis account as a defining rule of marriage. Need proof? Just close your eyes, open your Old Testament, and put your finger down. Chances are you'll find an example of polygamy. Polygamy was not banned by Jewish leaders until the 11th century, by Rabbi Gershom ben Judah. When Jesus quoted the creation story, he was not reminding them that marriage was between one man and one woman. He was reminding them that God created us for each other, for companionship. That's how they understood that passage. He was telling them that sending your companion, whom God joined to you, away to live on the streets (and usually forced into prostitution), was unloving and wrong. Even Paul understood the Genesis passage that way:

> "Therefore a man shall leave his father and mother and hold fast to his wife (gyne, a woman, married or unmarried), and the two shall become one flesh (sarx, physical body or nature)." This mystery (mysterion, hidden thing, secret, mystery) is profound, and I am saying that it refers to Christ and the church. However, let each one of you love his wife as himself, and let the wife see that she respects her husband. (Ephesians 5:31-33)

God joined you, damn it. Don't tear yourselves apart. Just like how God and his people should not be separated, you should not treat your companion unlovingly. We were created for companionship and love, and we screwed up. The way women have been treated since the fall of humanity is sinful and disgusting. Issues should not be decided by the strength of one's arms, but by the love one has for others. Nevertheless, sin is real, and humanity as a whole will never fully behave the way we were created to. But as Christians, we are called to resemble the true *nature* of creation, and not its distortion. We are to strive to live according to the way we were created. God intended us to enjoy each other as equals and to acknowledge Him and his creation. Our goal should be to return to that state as best we can.

## The Image of God

*"The story begins with God creating humanity in His image, male and female. Two distinct but complementary creatures, made for each other. Together, man and woman were fashioned to reflect the image and likeness of God. Male and female, together, are the fullest picture of the image of God in creation. That's why they need each other." (Glenn Stanton, My Crazy Imperfect Christian Family: Living Out Your Faith with Those Who Know You Best)*

If God's divine plan for marriage, according to the Genesis creation account, is one man, one woman, and the image of God is only realized with this union, then the man alone or the woman alone does not reflect the image of God. Why then does Paul recommend not entering into the divine plan of marriage? Now, Paul was a man of many opinions, and he wasn't afraid to let them be known. However, when writing to the Corinthians, he made it clear to his audience that some of what he was saying was his opinion and not from the Lord (1 Corinthians 7:12). What Paul wrote was intended for a specific audience, at a specific time, and for a specific purpose. He was addressing issues that people were dealing with at their current time.

*To the unmarried and the widows I say that it is good for them to remain single, as I am. But if they cannot exercise self-control, they should marry. For it is better to marry than to **burn with passion** (pyroo, burn, to be on fire). (1 Corinthians 7:8-9 ESV)*

You may recall from our previous studies that Paul was addressing cult prostitution in chapter 7. He had just finished stating that it is better to get married than to be tempted to worship a false god through sex with a cult prostitute. In verses 8-9, he is telling the Corinthians that it's also good to stay single. However, it's better to get married than to get drawn into idol worship and perish (I think we can assume he means something similar to "be destroyed"; God takes idolatry seriously). As noted above, Paul did like to give his opinions, so he may not have been establishing doctrine here, but why would someone who understood Genesis so well say that it's best not to get married? He knows that only together do we form the "perfect picture of the image of God," right? Why does he think it is permissible to not follow God's plan and not enter into the relationship that reflects the image of God? Is it possible that Paul recognized a divine plan from creation that was different from the divine plan the church recognizes today? If the plan from Genesis is as important as the Church believes, how can it simply be disregarded by Paul? If only Jesus would weigh in on the issue. Maybe then we could understand it:

> *The disciples said to him, "If such is the case of a man with his wife, it is better not to marry." But he said to them, "Not everyone can receive this saying, but only those to whom it is given (didomi, give, grant, bestow, supply). For there are eunuchs who have been so from birth, and there are eunuchs who have been made eunuchs by men, and there are eunuchs who have made themselves eunuchs for the sake of the kingdom of heaven. Let the one who is able to receive this receive it." (Matthew 19:10-12 ESV)*

Jesus had just told the Pharisees that divorce was unloving. So someone says, "Wait a minute, if we can't ditch our wives, then we shouldn't get married at all!" Jesus answered and said that singleness is not for everyone. It's something people are granted (*didomi*). Like eunuchs, some are created that way, some have been forced into it, and some decided to be that way for the sake of loving God. And he tops it off by basically saying, "You do you boo." So, who "grants" or "gives" this personality trait to the person who "receives" or "accepts" it? If they're born with it, God does (it comes *naturally*). If it is forced upon someone, people do. And if they choose it, they themselves do. We can apply that in so many ways. In the case of God's image, it shows us that Jesus (God Himself) says some people are born to not conform to what the church believes is the "fullest picture of the image of God in creation" (Stanton).

Marriage between only one male and one female, for life, was NOT God's plan for creation. LOVE was God's plan for creation. He created people in different ways. He grants and gives (*didomi*) them personality traits, abilities, and preferences, just like he does with the rest of *nature*. God's image is not based on sexual preferences. It is based on companionship. God is not a man. God is not a woman. God is a companionship of three: *Yahweh, Yeshua, and Holy Spirit.* God is *Elohim.* They are *joined* together as one, in harmony with each other.

> *In the beginning, God (Elohim, plural Hebrew word for God) created the heavens and the earth.*

In the beginning, God saw that it was not good for man to be alone, so he created a companion for him, just as He had for

Himself. In the beginning, God did not create or establish rules around that companionship. Marriage as we know it today is a civil institution, not a creation of God. I'm not arguing against getting married. I have been married for 20 years and have never been happier. But marriage is just a piece of paper. True, biblical companionship, as given to us by Elohim, is based on *love*. Why can't three people love each other? God is three. Why can't two men love each other? It's how God created them.

> *For his invisible attributes, namely, his eternal power and divine nature, have been clearly perceived, ever since the creation of the world, in the things that have been made. (Romans 1:20 ESV)*

It's *NATURAL.*

## CONCLUSION

So, is life just one big free-for-all? Should I be teaching my children to go have as much sex as they want regardless of whether they ever get married? Not at all. Actions have consequences. In everything you do, there's an element of risk and reward. When you decide to get in the driver's seat of a car, you risk injury or death, but the reward is you get to your destination faster. If you decide to walk instead, it will take much longer, but the reward is that it's safer. We do what we can to make wise decisions, mitigate risks (use a seatbelt), and do it in a way that comes *naturally* in our cultural setting. The Israelite people had lots of babies. It was normal, and the communities helped raise them. It's different today. Having a child with no way to care for it is difficult. When you have a baby without a companion to help out, it can make life very difficult. When you have sex, at least for a male and female, one of the risks is pregnancy. Before you take what this book says and run with it, consider the risks of whatever you choose to do and decide if it's worth it. If the action you're considering is done in a loving way, and you're comfortable with the risks, then it is your decision to make. If there's any element of being unloving toward either God or others, then make a better choice. If something becomes an obsession, it becomes an idol, and I think we know what God thinks about that. It's kind of a theme of His. So let's summarize what we have learned:

- God is the all-powerful, inerrant creator of the universe
- God created humanity in their image (*Elohim*)
- He created humanity to love Him
- He created humanity to love others
- Humanity desired more and fell from God's grace (*Hamad, Epithymia*)
- Humanity created idols and destroyed God's temple, our body (*Porneia*)
- God became man as a sacrifice to pay for humanity's betrayal
- God inspired humanity to document His words and teachings
- God wanted humanity to worship and acknowledge Him
- Humanity took those teachings and twisted His words
- Humanity wanted instead to control all sexual behavior
- Humanity turned God's Church into a business
- God is pleading for His Church to **bring Him back** into the scriptures we have distorted.

We have lessened God's demand and expectation for our love by redefining words that were meant to portray the importance of keeping Him first. We replaced those words with a phrase and concept that has done nothing but divide the church, cause shame and guilt where there should be none, and turned people away from the true message of Jesus Christ. We should be ashamed of ourselves. What was meant to warn us about idolatry and the danger of turning away from God has become a rabbit trail of sexual thou-shalt-nots. We then turned our churches into businesses and made the claim that our Bibles are the inerrant holders of absolute truth, reducing the need for faith. As a church, we need to have a discussion. The facts presented in this book directly contradict what has been taught since evangelical churches started. My book is not inerrant, but it's useful. My current church is full of loving, caring individuals who want deeply to know God and to help others. I believe they will answer the call to have this discussion. So much of our study has been based on words the apostle Paul used, so I think it is appropriate to conclude by letting him speak for himself:

> *If I speak in the tongues of men and of angels, but have not love, I am a noisy gong or a clanging cymbal. And if I have prophetic powers, and understand all mysteries and all knowledge, and if I have all faith, so as to remove mountains, but have not love, I am nothing. If I give away all I have, and if I deliver up my body to be burned, but have not love, I gain nothing. Love is patient and kind; love does not envy or boast; it is not arrogant or rude. It does not insist on its own way; it is not irritable or resentful; it does not rejoice at wrongdoing, but rejoices with the truth. Love bears all things, believes all things, hopes all things, endures all things. Love never ends. As for prophecies, they will pass away; as for*

*tongues, they will cease; as for knowledge, it will pass away. For we know in part and we prophesy in part, but when the perfect comes, the partial will pass away. When I was a child, I spoke like a child, I thought like a child, I reasoned like a child. When I became a man, I gave up childish ways. For now we see in a mirror dimly, but then face to face.* ***Now I know in part; then I shall know fully, even as I have been fully known. So now faith, hope, and love abide, these three; but the greatest of these is love.*** *(1 Corinthians 13)*

## People of the church. We need to talk.

## ACKNOWLEDGMENTS

This was not an easy book to complete. Due to the subject matter, it was necessary to keep it secret from everyone except my wife. Two years of tough conversations about what we were learning, and how it would affect us, were both brutal and freeing. My wife and I would isolate ourselves in a room with the doors closed, and hash out our traditions. Our children often wondered what was going on, which led to some great conversation time with them. I want to acknowledge the patience my wife, Lydia, has had with me for these two years. And I want to thank her for not hesitating to let me know when I was not communicating clearly. I also want to thank my friends (withholding names for privacy, but you know who you are) for offering their suggestions and improvements for the book. They made this book better, and I am eternally grateful.